VOLUME 10

LOCKHEED
SR-71/YF-12 BLACKBIRDS

BY DENNIS R. JENKINS

PUBLISHERS AND WHOLESALERS

Published by
Specialty Press Publishers and Wholesalers
11481 Kost Dam Road
North Branch, MN 55056
United States of America
(612) 583-3239

Distributed in the UK and Europe by
Airlife Publishing Ltd.
101 Longden Road
Shrewsbury
SY3 9EB
England

ISBN 0-933424-85-X

Designed by Greg Compton

Printed in the United States of America

TABLE OF CONTENTS

THE LOCKHEED SR-71/YF-12 BLACKBIRDS

PREFACE

On 26 April 1962, Lockheed test pilot Lou Schalk took the first flight in an aircraft at a classified desert test facility in Nevada. The aircraft was far more advanced than anything in the sky, and when made public several years later, would capture the world's fascination like few other aircraft ever have. Three distinct variants were eventually manufactured, but surprisingly, none of them ever had an official name. Unofficially, they have all been referred to as "Blackbirds" and "Habu," the fastest, highest flying air-breathing aircraft in the world. The Lockheed model number of the first variant was A-12, but by a sort of inspired perversity it came to be called OXCART, a code name also applied to the program under which it was developed. The other two variants carried the Air Force designations YF-12 and SR-71.

Over the years there have been many books published on various aspects of the Blackbird's development and operations. The first attempt to tell the complete story was Jay Miller's *Aerofax Minigraph #1: Lockheed SR-71*, which still does a credible job even though it is over ten years old, and published before many of the facts were officially released. Miller did an even better job in *Lockheed Skunk Works: The First Fifty Years*, published in 1993. Col. Richard H. Graham, a former SR-71 pilot and 9th Strategic Reconnaissance Wing Commander, gives an excellent look at the operations of the Blackbird in *SR-71 Revealed: The Inside Story*. James Goodall provided excellent photographic coverage in Squadron Signal's *SR-71 Blackbird*. Interestingly, the short-lived YF-12 interceptor still seems largely forgotten.

The sixties were a time of worry in the United States. The Cold War was in full bloom, and the United States was spending a fortune attempting to find a technological solution to fighting the Soviets. While our expected adversaries were busy building realistic bomb shelters for the inhabitants of Moscow, the United States was building the Distant Early Warning (DEW) line, the PINE TREE line, and hundreds of Bomarc and Nike Hercules surface-to-air missile sites around the northern perimeter of the continent. There was always a question of how well this technology would work (not all that well in retrospect) and also the fear that the Soviets would simply build aircraft capable of attacking from directions other than from over the North Pole.

Interceptors could answer this envisioned threat since they could be based almost anywhere, and moved as required. The first truly workable interceptor capable of countering modern bombers was the Convair F-106 Delta Dart, and for its era it had a good combination of speed, weapons, and fire control system. But the Air Force wanted to intercept the Soviets further from the American coast. To do this a great deal more speed and range would be needed, since radar is inherently

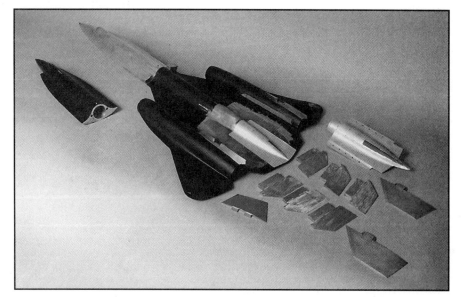

This wind tunnel model of the Blackbird shows the differences between the variants. The nose on the model is of the SR-71, while the extra nose section shows the cut-off chines of the YF-12. The rear fuselage on the model is from the A-12/YF-12 while the other rear fuselage is from the SR-71. Various vertical stabilizers and ventral fins are shown behind the model. (Tony Landis collection)

limited in range, and could only provide so much warning.

There had been an attempt to build a dedicated high-speed interceptor in the Republic XF-103, but that program had ended when Alexander Kartveli's creation proved to be far too advanced for existing technology. Logically, North American's XF-108 Rapier long-range escort fighter could have been modified into a credible interceptor, but that program was cancelled along with the B-70 it was supposed to accompany. Another attempt was made in Canada with the Avro CF-105 Arrow, but it too was cancelled. But Lockheed already had a high-speed, long-range platform available. The A-12 spy plane was being developed for the CIA, but Skunk Work's Kelly Johnson managed to get an Air Force contract to demonstrate its potential as an interceptor.

Unfortunately, it was not to be. Even now it is difficult to tell how sincere all the participants were in their desire to build an interceptor. Although the Air Force considered ordering 93 production F-12Bs, it is highly unlikely they could ever have afforded to build or operate them. Lockheed would definitely have liked to manufacture the aircraft since the publicity would have been priceless. But the aircraft was largely hand-built,

The Blackbirds were developed long before the advent of fly-by-wire control systems and still used a series of cables and push-pull rods to transmit the pilot's desires to the flight control surfaces. The Blackbirds

and it is questionable if it would have been profitable. By this time the CIA was out of the picture, so it is doubtful that they really cared.

Only a single YF-12A still exists. It adorns the modern air wing of the Air Force Museum at Wright-Patterson AFB, Ohio. The thought of flight lines full of these hauntingly beautiful aircraft would have been a sight to behold.

I would like to thank Mick Roth, Tony Landis, Denny Lombard, Troy Downen, Jim Eastham, Steve Ishmael, Fred Johnsen, Jay Miller and Brenda Anderson for their help in assembling this publication.

TERMINOLOGY

One term used by the Blackbird crews deserves a special mention. The story here is paraphrased from the preface of *SR-71 Revealed: The Inside Story* since I believe that Col. Graham probably knows it as well or better than anybody. Within their own community, the Blackbirds and its crews were called "Habu"

(pronounced "Haw-boo"). The term originated from the time when the first Blackbirds arrived on Okinawa and the residents indicated that the cobra-shaped aircraft reminded them of an indigenous snake called the Habu. The snake was not generally considered aggressive, but when backed into a corner it could, and would bite, always painfully and sometimes deadly. Thus the Blackbird became known locally as the Habu, and the crews soon adopted the term also.

And, when the U-2s arrived at Beale AFB in July 1976 after being transferred from their own base at Davis-Monthan AFB, they did not seem inclined to call the SR-71 either "Habu" or "Blackbird." They proceeded to come up with their own term, referring to the SR-71 in a disparaging manner as "The Sled." The SR-71 crews accepted this as a friendly camaraderie, and have even advertised themselves as "Sled Drivers" on occasion.

DENNIS R. JENKINS
1997

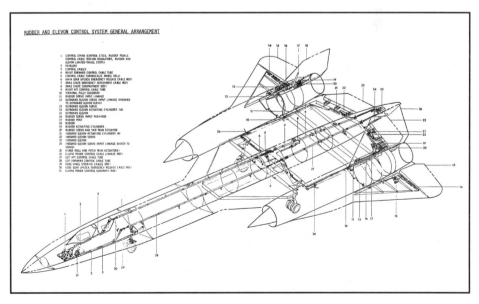

RUDDER AND ELEVON CONTROL SYSTEM GENERAL ARRANGEMENT

only had six primary control surfaces – two inner elevons, two outer elevons, and two rudders. Due to the pressures experienced at Mach 3+, each outer elevon had a remarkable 14 separate actuators. (U.S. Air Force)

SUNTAN, GUSTO AND KINGFISH

The early 1950s were a period of rapid technological advance for United States military aviation. In February 1953 Chance-Vought delivered the last propeller-driven fighter (an F4U Corsair). Three months later, North American delivered the YF-100 Super Sabre, the first fighter capable of supersonic speeds in level flight.

In March 1953, the Central Intelligence Agency (CIA) issued a set of specifications for a new reconnaissance aircraft capable of an altitude of 70,000 feet and a range of 1,750 miles. It was believed that the high operational ceiling would enable the aircraft to penetrate Soviet airspace at subsonic speeds in relative safety. The aircraft would carry a single crew member and 100-700 pounds of mission equipment, and eventually resulted in the development of the Lockheed U-2. The aircraft became operational in June 1956, and would remain an invaluable source of overflight information for almost four years, until 1 May 1960, when Francis Gary Powers was shot down near Sverdlovsk.

However, even as the U-2 was being tested and used operationally over the Soviet Union, it was obvious that a faster and higher flying aircraft would be needed to stay ahead of the increasing surface-to-air (SAM) missile threat. Around this time the Air Force and NACA (later NASA) were investigating the feasibility of using liquid hydrogen to power high-altitude aircraft. A contract was issued to the Garrett Corporation to design a hydrogen-fueled jet engine called REX. During 1956, Lockheed used the proposed REX engines in studies of the CL-325 aircraft, but on 18 October 1956 the Air Force decided that the engine and aircraft were too complex and cancelled the effort. Nevertheless, Kelly Johnson appreciated the potential of liquid hydrogen as a fuel, and offered to build the Air Force two aircraft based on the CL-325 design that would cruise at Mach 2.5 and 98,000 feet, with a range of over 2,500 miles. The Air Force, looking to upstage the CIA and build the U-2 follow-on, was very interested.

This was the beginning of the most ambitious of the liquid hydrogen studies. Code named SUNTAN, the study eventually spent approximately $300 million, but was cancelled before any aircraft could be built. The final SUNTAN design was 290 feet long with a 98 foot wingspan and had a take-off weight of 358,500 pounds including a crew of two and 1,500 pounds of mission equipment. Even though it was never built, the technology developed for SUNTAN contributed to the eventual development of the Centaur upper stage rocket.

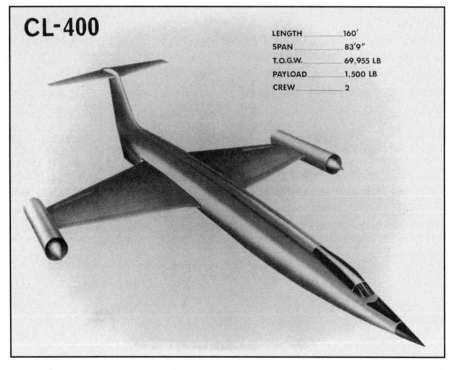

CL-400

LENGTH	160'
SPAN	83'9"
T.O.G.W.	69,955 LB
PAYLOAD	1,500 LB
CREW	2

The CL-400-10 developed under Project SUNTAN is one of the few major projects at Skunk Works that did not reach the full-scale hardware stage. This liquid hydrogen-fueled aircraft would have used two Pratt & Whitney 304-2 hydrogen expander engines to reach Mach 2.5 at 90,000 feet. The total liquid hydrogen capacity was 32,550 gallons (only 19,235 pounds). (Lockheed)

In 1956 the CIA appointed Richard M. Bissell, Jr., who had been the CIA's program manager for the U-2, to oversee the development of an advanced reconnaissance aircraft. Studies under the code name GUSTO investigated a new subsonic high-altitude aircraft that was designed from the beginning to be as invisible to radar as possible (the term "stealth" had not yet been applied to aircraft). Most of the Lockheed GUSTO designs took the form of large flying wings capable of of altitudes in excess of 70,000 feet. Using then-existing material technology it was quickly discovered that aircraft weight rose faster than its radar cross-section got smaller. A new approach would obviously need to be found.

In the fall of 1957 the CIA arranged with Skunk Works to determine how the probability of shooting down an aircraft varied with respect to the its speed, altitude, and radar cross-section. This analysis demonstrated that supersonic speed greatly reduced the chances of detection by radar. The probability of being shot down was not reduced to zero, but it was evident that high speed overflight was worth serious consideration. Attention now focused increasingly on the possibility of building an aircraft which could fly at extremely high speeds as well as high altitudes. Working with Kelly Johnson, Bissell drew up the basic requirements for a U-2 successor: a low radar cross-section aircraft with a Mach 3+ cruising speed at altitudes in excess of 80,000 feet. In late 1957 Lockheed and Convair were officially informed of the general requirements, and began developing possible designs using company funds.

Bissell realized that development

and production of such an aircraft would be exceedingly expensive, and that there would be a great deal of skepticism about whether the project could succeed at all. To secure the necessary funds for such a program, Bissell believed he would need the support of the most believable experts he could find. Accordingly, Bissell put together a panel consisting of two distinguished authorities on aerodynamics and one physicist, with E. M. Land of the Polaroid Corporation as chairman. Between 1957 and 1959 this panel met six times, usually in Land's office in Cambridge.

Kelly Johnson's "Skunk Works" began designing an aircraft that would cruise at Mach 3.0 at altitudes above 90,000 feet. On 23 July 1958 he presented his new high-speed concept to Land's advisory

committee, which expressed interest in the approach he was taking. At the same meeting, Navy representatives presented a concept for a high-altitude reconnaissance vehicle using an inflatable rubber ramjet-powered vehicle that would be lifted to high altitude by a balloon. The vehicle would then be dropped and powered by an expendable rocket to a speed where the ramjets could produce thrust. Lockheed was asked to evaluate this concept, and three weeks later, after receiving more details from the Navy representatives, Kelly Johnson made some quick calculations that showed that the design was impractical because the balloon would have to be a mile in diameter to lift the vehicle, which in turn would need a wing surface greater than 6,223 sq.ft. to carry the payload!

Archangel II was the second in the "A" series of design studies conducted under the OXCART project. This configuration was powered by two turbojet engines under the wings at mid-span and two ramjets on the wingtips. Unlike the competing Convair FISH configurations this design had no radar-defeating features. (Lockheed)

Clarence L. "Kelly" Johnson (27 February 1910-21 December 1990), Lockheed Senior Vice President, and first Director of the Lockheed Advanced Development Company (LADC), now known simply as "Skunk Works." Much more than an engineer, and certainly more than a mere manager, Kelly Johnson was one of the greatest, and possibly the last, great aviation visionaries. His legacy includes the P-80, T-33, F-94, F-104, U-2, and the Blackbirds, amongst others. (Lockheed)

By September 1958, Lockheed had studied a number of possible configurations, some based on ramjet engines, others with both ramjets and turbojets. Engineers at Skunk Works referred to these concepts as ARCHANGEL-1, ARCHANGEL-2, etc., a carryover from the original code name of the ANGEL given to the U-2 during its development. These designs soon became simply A-1, A-2, etc.

In September 1958, the Land committee met again to decide which concepts were most likely to lead to a production aircraft. Among those rejected were the Navy's inflatable ramjet-powered aircraft, an unsolicited Boeing proposal for a 190-foot-long hydrogen-powered inflatable aircraft, and a Lockheed design for a hydrogen-powered aircraft derived from the SUNTAN studies. The committee also examined two other Lockheed designs – a tailless subsonic aircraft with a very-low-radar cross-section (the G2A from the GUSTO studies) and a new supersonic design (the A-2). The committee did not accept either Lockheed design, the former because of its low speed and the latter because of it dependence on exotic penta-borane fuel for its ramjets. The committee approved the continuation of Convair's work on a ramjet-powered Mach 4.0 "parasite" that would be launched from a specially configured version of the proposed B-58B bomber. The Convair design was called FISH.

Two months later, after reviewing the Convair proposal and yet another Lockheed design (the A-3), the Land committee concluded in late November 1958 that it would indeed be feasible to build an aircraft whose speed and altitude would make radar tracking and interception difficult or impossible. The committee recommended that the CIA ask President Eisenhower to approve funding to enter detailed design. The CIA requested, and was granted, $100 million to develop and manufacture 12 aircraft.

Lockheed and Convair were asked to submit detailed proposals, and during the first half of 1959 both companies worked to reduce the radar cross-section of their designs. Most tracking radars in the late 1950s swept a band of sky 30-45° wide and 360° in circumference. Any object in this area reflected the radar pulse in a manner directly proportional to its size. This return appeared on the radar screen as a spot or blip, and the persistence of this blip on the radar screen depended on the strength of the radar return, with blips from larger objects being brighter and remaining on the screen longer. During the late 1950s and early 1960s, a human operator watched the radar screen and kept track of the blips that indicated aircraft within the radar's field of view. It was surmised that a high altitude object moving two to three times faster than a normal aircraft would produce such a small blip with so little persistence that a radar operator would have great difficulty tracking it, if indeed he could even see it. To take advantage of this it was determined that an aircraft must fly at approximately 90,000 feet and have a radar cross-section of less than 10 square meters.

The Blackbirds had rugged airframes. These drawings show the aircraft stations (frames) that were located approximately 20 inches apart. The fuselage and nacelle station designations corresponds to inches aft of the nose. (U.S. Air Force)

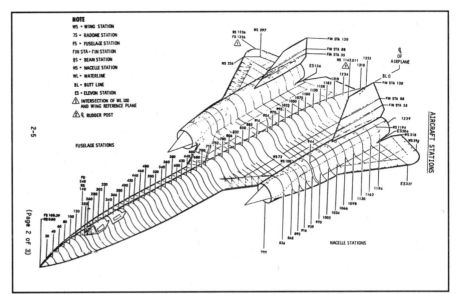

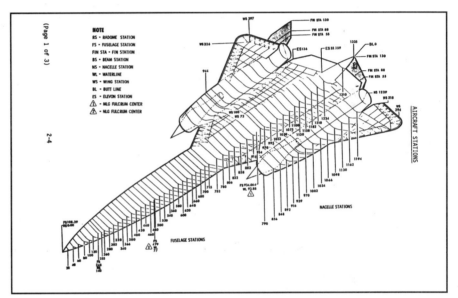

By the summer of 1959, both contractors had completed their proposals. Lockheed submitted a design for a ground-launched aircraft known as the A-11. The Pratt & Whitney J58 turbojet-powered aircraft would have a speed of Mach 3.2 at 90,000 feet, a range of 3,200 miles, and a first flight in January 1961. Kelly Johnson had refused to compromise the aerodynamics of this design in order to achieve a lower radar cross-section, and the A-11 presented a substantially larger target than the much smaller parasite aircraft being proposed by Convair.

The Convair proposal called for a small ramjet-powered reconnaissance vehicle to be air-launched from a specially configured B-58B Super Hustler. The FISH vehicle, a radical lifting-body with a very small radar cross-section, would fly Mach 4.2 at 90,000 feet and have a range of 3,900 miles. Two Marquardt ramjets would power its dash over the target area, and once FISH decelerated, two J58 turbojets would bring it back to base. The ramjet exit nozzles and wing edges would be constructed of Pyroceram, a ceramic material that could withstand the high temperatures and also absorb some of the radar signals. Convair stated that the FISH could be ready by January 1961.

Convair's proposal depended on two high-risk factors. First and foremost was the unproven technology of the ramjet engines. Since ramjet

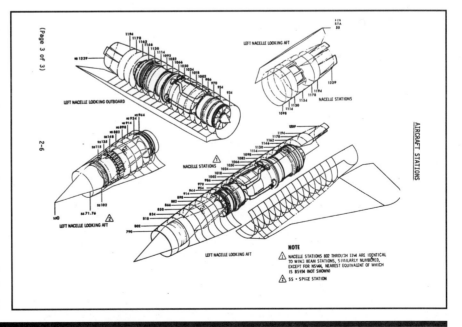

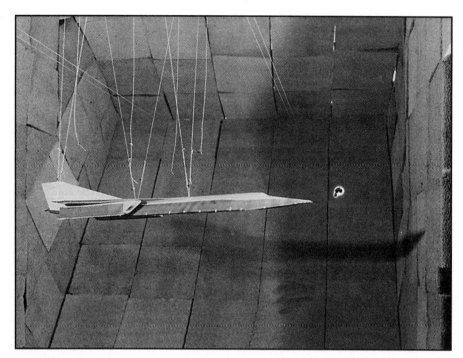

The Archangel designs were extensively tested in the Lockheed anachoic chamber. Here the A-10 shows its high-wing and single tail design. This presented several problems, notably excessive heating at high speeds due to air trapped between the nacelles and fuselage under the wing. The single tail also provided less than ideal directional stability. (Lockheed)

engines had only been tested in wind tunnels, there was no available data to confirm that they would work in the proposed application. The second uncertainty was the B-58B bomber that was supposed to achieve Mach 2.2 before launching FISH above 35,000 feet since it was still in preliminary development and was not a confirmed and funded project.

Convair's proposal suffered a major setback in June 1959, when the Air Force cancelled the B-58B project and no other aircraft appeared capable of serving as a launch vehicle. The Convair proposal was therefore unusable, but the Lockheed design with its high radar cross-section was also unacceptable to the Land committee. On 14 July 1959, the committee rejected both designs. Lockheed continued to work on developing a design that would be less vulnerable to detection, and Convair received a new CIA contract to design an air-breathing aircraft that would meet the general specifications being followed by Lockheed.

By the late summer of 1959, both Convair and Lockheed had completed new designs. Convair's entry was a delta-wing planform using stainless steel honeycomb skin and incorporating a crew capsule system which eliminated the need for the pilot to wear a pressurized suit. The Mach 3.2 KINGFISH had two J58 engines buried inside the fuselage, which significantly reduced the radar cross-section.

Lockheed's new A-12 entry was much like the A-11 but tuned to reduce the radar cross-section. Edward Purcell of the Land committee had suggested adding a small amount of cesium to the fuel to decrease the radar cross-section of the afterburner plume, an improvement Lockheed adopted. In an effort to save weight Lockheed decided to use a titanium alloy to construct the A-12 since traditional lightweight metals such as aluminum were out of the question because they could not stand the heat generated at Mach 3.2, and steel was rejected because of its weight.

On 20 August 1959, Lockheed and Convair submitted their proposals to a joint Department of Defense, Air Force, and CIA selection panel. The two aircraft were generally similar in performance characteristics and the Lockheed design was selected based mainly on cost. The project was given the code name OXCART at the end of August 1959.

However, the selection panel remained concerned about the A-12's vulnerability to radar detection and on 14 September 1959 the CIA issued a four-month contract to Lockheed to proceed with anti-radar studies, aerodynamic structural tests, and engineering designs. It was during this radar testing that the OXCART received its characteristic cobra-like appearance. Lockheed came up with a theory that a continuously curving airframe would be difficult to track because it would present few corner reflections or sharp angles from which radar pulses could reflect (this is, interestingly, exactly the opposite of the theory that led to the straight-edged F-117).

To achieve this, curved extensions were added to the engine housings and leading edges of the wings, and eventually to the fuselage itself, creating a large chine on each side. At first Johnson was concerned that these additions might

impair the airworthiness of the plane, but wind tunnel testing determined that the chines actually contributed a slight aerodynamic benefit. Because titanium was very brittle and therefore difficult to bend the necessary curvature was achieved by combining small triangular-shaped pieces of titanium that were glued to the airframe with a special epoxy adhesive.

Only the first A-12 used the titanium chine fillets; all later Blackbirds used fillets and wing leading edges made from electrically resistive honeycomb plastic with a glass-fiber surface that would not melt at high speed. When struck by a radar pulse, the composite chines tended to absorb the pulse rather than reflect it. The greatest remaining area of concern in the A-12's radar cross-section was the two vertical stabilizers. To reduce radar reflections, Kelly Johnson canted the stabilizers 15° inward and fabricated them out of resin-impregnated high-temperature plastic materials. The only metal in each vertical stabilizer was a stainless steel pivot. The Air Force, which later ordered several versions of the OXCART aircraft for its own use, was reluctant to use the laminated vertical stabilizers, and generally flew with titanium ones instead.

For most of the Blackbird's career it was started using a special cart powered by a pair of modified automobile engines. Originally these were Buick V-8 automotive engines, leading to the carts taking on the same name. Later the Buick engines were replaced by big-block Chevys. Through a series of gears the engines drove a vertical shaft that extended through the top of the cart and into the bottom of the nacelle to the J58s starting gears. The reason for this direct-drive starter was simply because there were no air starting carts capable of supplying a sufficient volume of air to rotate the J58 engine. Eventually the SR-71 shelters at Beale were equipped with large compressed air tanks to rotate the starter adapter. The "Buicks" continued to be used at remote sites. (Troy Downen)

THE CIA'S 2 OXCART

According to the specifications, OXCART was to achieve a speed of Mach 3.2 (2,064 knots or 0.57 miles per second, which would make it slightly faster than a 0.30 rifle bullet), have a range of 4,120 nautical miles, and reach altitudes of 84,500 to 97,500 feet. The new aircraft would thus be more than five times as fast as the U-2 and would go almost three miles higher. But by mid-January 1960 the changes needed to reduce the radar cross-section also led to a reduction in the aircraft's performance.

To overcome this, Lockheed proposed reducing the aircraft's weight by 1,000 pounds and increasing the fuel load by 2,000 pounds, making it possible to achieve the target altitude of 90,000 feet. Afterward, Kelly Johnson noted in the ARCHANGEL project log: "We have no performance margins left; so this project, instead of being 10 times as hard as any-thing we have done, is 12 times as hard. This matches the design number and is obviously right."

On 26 January the CIA authorized the construction of 12 OXCART aircraft with the contract being signed on 11 February 1960. Lockheed's cost estimate was $96.6 million for 12 aircraft, but technological difficulties eventually more than doubled the original estimate. Designed with slide rules in the days before computers, the Blackbirds would fly at altitudes where the ambient air temperature was -70°F. Despite this seemingly frigid

This wind tunnel model (both models were "flown" in the tunnel on their sides, rolled 90 degrees from normal flight) is remarkably close to the final configuration. The final design featured a complex twist to the leading edge of the outboard wing panels and slightly revised chines on the nose to cure the pitch instability. Although more difficult to manufacture, these changes provided a fix with the fewest compromises to performance. (Lockheed)

Wind tunnel testing of the A-12 design revealed a pitch instability that was worrisome to Kelly Johnson and the design team. One of the first attempts to cure this instability involved fitting large canards. Although these cured the instability, they disturbed the air flow into the engine inlets, and also had an adverse affect on the "stealth" characteristics of the design. (Lockheed)

environment, the nose of the aircraft would heat up to 800°F, the windshield to over 600°F, while the exhaust section behind the engines would reach over 1,200°F.

Since every pound of weight was critical, adequate insulation was out of the question and the inside of the aircraft would be like a moderately hot oven. The pilot would have to wear a full pressure suit with its own cooling apparatus, pressure control, and oxygen supply. The fuel tanks, which occupied most of the internal volume of the aircraft, would heat up to 350°F. This dictated a special low vapor pressure fuel (JP-7), and the tanks themselves were inerted with nitrogen to prevent the possibility of explosion. The fuel was also used as a heat sink to cool various parts of the aircraft.

Insulation on the aircraft's intricate wiring soon became brittle, resulting in short circuits and electronic failures. Although improved insulations were found, this remained a problem throughout OXCART's lifetime. Lockheed also had to search long and hard for hydraulic fluid that would not vaporize at high speed but would still be usable at low altitudes. Finding a suitable hydraulic pump was just as difficult. Literally every part on the A-12 had to be developed from scratch.

The choice of titanium for the airframe also presented some challenges. After evaluating many materials, Lockheed chose an alloy of titanium (BetA-120/Ti-13V-11Cr-3A1) characterized by great strength, relatively light weight, and good high temperature characteristics. Obtaining sufficient quantities of titanium of a quality suitable for fabricating aircraft

One of the A-12s nearing final assembly in Burbank. The vertical stabilizers and outer wing panels have not been fitted yet, providing an idea of how the aircraft is assembled. The large object in the foreground is one of the special $100,000 trailers used to transport the fuselage to Groom Lake. (Lockheed)

components proved very difficult. First, most of the world's known titanium reserves at the time were located in the Soviet Union. Second, methods for maintaining good quality control during the refining and milling of titanium were not fully developed and up to 80% of the early deliveries from Titanium Metals Corporation had to be

The last A-12 (60-6939) in final assembly. Lockheed completed the aircraft, then removed the outer wing panels, nose, and vertical stabilizers prior to transporting them to Groom Lake. Interestingly, this A-12 shows the metal vertical stabilizer that was replaced with a high-temperature plastic composite unit to improve the radar-defeating performance of the aircraft. Barely visible on the extreme left is the first SR-71 (64-17950). (Lockheed)

The first A-12 (60-6924) in final checkout at Burbank. Only the first A-12 used titanium fuselage chines and wing leading edges, as shown by the overall metal finish on this aircraft. All later aircraft used high-temperature plastic composites for these surfaces. (Lockheed)

rejected. It was not until 1961, when TMC officials were informed of the national security objectives and high priority of the OXCART program, that quality control problems with the titanium supply ended. Even after sufficient high-quality titanium was received, Lockheed's difficulties were not over.

One of the virtues of titanium was its extreme hardness, but this created difficulties in machining and shaping the material. Drills which worked well on aluminum disintegrated and new ones had to be devised. It was also found that wrenches and other tools that were plated with certain metals had a detrimental effect on the titanium, and special tools had to be purchased. Assembly-line production was basically impossible and each of the small OXCART fleet was more-or-less hand built.

The last A-12 (60-6939) in final assembly. Large plastic covers were placed over the chine areas to prevent damage by workers during the assembly process. The cockpit canopy has yet to be fitted, and the large opening behind the cockpit is the "Q" bay used to house the photographic equipment. The first M-21 mother-ship is immediately behind this A-12, separated by a security screen. (Lockheed)

WARBIRDTECH
S E R I E S

From the very beginning, it was clear that Lockheed could not test OXCART at its Burbank facility where the runway was too short and too exposed to the public. The ideal testing site would be far removed from metropolitan areas, away from civil and military airways, easily accessible by air, blessed with good weather, capable of accommodating large numbers of personnel, near an Air Force installation, and have a runway at least 8,000 feet long. But no such place was to be found. Ten Air Force bases programmed for closure were considered, but none provided the necessary security, and annual operating costs at most of them would be unacceptable. Edwards Air Force Base in California seemed a more likely candidate, but in the end it too was passed over. Instead an abandoned auxiliary training field at Groom Lake, Nevada, was selected. This test site has since been known as "Area 51," "The Ranch," and "The Test Site."

Delays in obtaining the J58 engines caused the postponement of the final assembly of the first A-12, and eventually, Lockheed and the CIA decided to begin testing without waiting for the J58 engines. In their place would be J75 engines, designed for the Convair F-106, that would allow testing of the A-12 at

It was fortunate that JP-7 proved to be relatively non-flammable under most conditions due to its high vapor pressure. On the ground the Blackbirds leaked like a sieve. This chart shows "acceptable" leak rates of up to 60 drops per minute per side per fuel tank in certain locations. A lot of spilled fuel was almost always present under a Blackbird that had been sitting for any length of time. (U.S. Air Force)

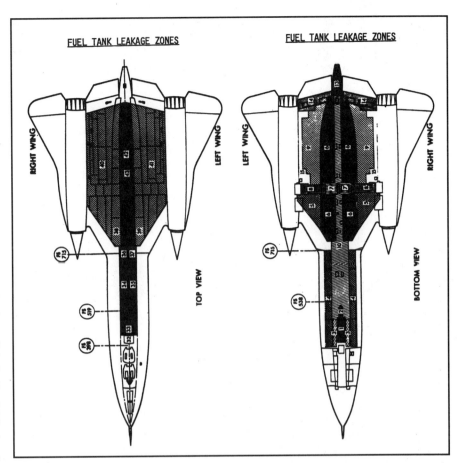

TABLE OF FUEL TANK LEAKAGE LIMITS

ZONE	ZONE DESCRIPTION	MAX. LEAKAGE ALLOWABLE
1	NLG Wheel Well	10 Drops/Minute/Side
2	NLG Trailing Door Compartment	30 Drops/Minute
3	E-Bay and R-Bay	25 Drops/Minute/Bay
4	Left and Right, Forward and Aft, Mission Equipment Bays	25 Drops/Minute/Bay
5	Fwd Lower Wing, Including Fwd Wall of MLG Wheel Well	150cc/Minute/Side
6	Fuselage Fillet Area	Leakage unimportant, but no single leak exceeding 50 Drops/Minute/Side
7	Inboard MLG Wheel Well (Excluding Fwd Wall of MLG Wheel Well)	5 Drops/Minute/Side Leaks not permitted in fuel plumbing.
8	Outboard MLG Wheel Well (Excluding Fwd Wall of MLG Wheel Well)	Dampness, no dripping permitted. Leaks not permitted in fuel plumbing.
9	Aft, Lower Wing	60 Drops/Minute/Side
10	Fuselage	Leakage unimportant, but no single leak exceeding 50 Drops/Minute
11	Top, Wing	Leakage unimportant, but no single leak exceeding 60 Drops/Minute/Side
12	Drag Chute Compartment	Dampness, puddling not permitted
13	Tailcone (excluding vent and dump line leakage)	10 Drops/Minute
14	Aft of Rear Beam	Leakage unimportant but no single leak exceeding 60 Drops/Minute/Side
15	Dry Bay Areas (outboard of tanks 6A and 6B)	950 cc/Minute/Side

WARNING

Observe the requirements of paragraph 2-11 when using this chart.

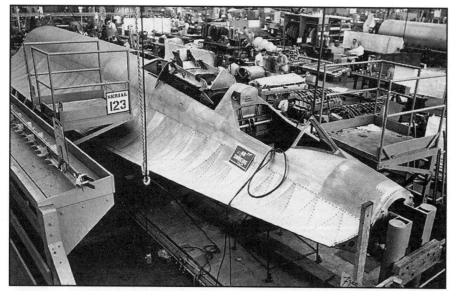

The third A-12 (60-6926) provides a view of the "Q" bay and cockpit area. This is the forward fuselage assembly area in Burbank. The forward fuselage was built-up separately from the aft fuselage and wings, and the two major subassemblies were joined on the final assembly line. Due to their unique nature, the Blackbirds were largely manufactured by hand, resulting in no two aircraft being truly identical. (Lockheed)

altitudes up to 50,000 feet and at speeds up to Mach 1.6.

The first A-12 was assembled and checked-out at Burbank during January and February 1962. Since it could not be flown to Groom Lake, the aircraft was partially disassembled and put on a specially designed trailer that cost nearly $100,000. A thorough survey of the route in June 1961 showed that a

(Above) This photograph both confirms and dispels rumors that have circulated for years that the A-12 could carry external payloads above the inboard wing panels. Due to excessive leakage of the A-12's wing tanks, Lockheed and the CIA were reluctant to fill them until the sealant could be improved. In an effort to not seriously impact the test program, external tanks were fitted to allow ground run-ups of the engines. This configuration was never flown. (Lockheed)

The first A-12 takes off on its first "official" flight on 30 April 1962 with Lou Shalk at the controls. This was actually the second flight of the aircraft, the first short hop having been accomplished five days before without an audience. This was somewhat fortunate since during the first flight the aircraft managed to shed almost all of the triangular titanium fillets that covered its nose chines. The chines were recovered from around the runway and hurriedly reattached to the aircraft. (Lockheed)

WARBIRDTECH
SERIES

package measuring 35 feet wide and 105 feet long could be transported without major difficulty. Appropriate arrangements were made with the police and local officials to safely transport the aircraft, without disclosing exactly what was in the odd-shaped container. The entire fuselage, minus wings, was loaded on the specially designed trailer and departed Burbank on 26 February 1962. It arrived at "The Ranch" two days later.

At Groom Lake the aircraft was reassembled and the J75 engines were installed, but the aircraft was still not ready to be tested. This delay was caused by leaking fuel tanks, a problem that would never be solved completely. Because the A-12's high speeds would heat the titanium airframe to more than 500°F, Lockheed designers had to make allowances for expansion. When the metal was cold, the expansion joints were at their widest. In the fuel tanks, these gaps were filled by pliable sealants, but

The A-12's cockpit was very conventional, shown here on 2 January 1962, before the periscopic sight had been installed at top center. Each of the Blackbird models featured a different cockpit arrangement, largely based on its mission and the number of crew. (Lockheed)

the JP-7 acted as a strong reducing agent that softened the sealants. When the aircraft was first fueled, 68 separate leaks developed. The fuel was drained, and Lockheed technicians stripped and replaced all the sealant, a tedious and time consuming procedure because the sealant required four curing cycles over a period of 30 to 54 hours. The engineers were never able to discover a sealing compound that was

The third A-12 (60-6926) clearly shows the triangular panels used on the leading edges of the wings and chines. The semi-circular area under the forward fuselage is the UHF antenna location. The early Blackbirds (A-12, M-21, and YF-12) had a rear fuselage that terminated even with the trailing edge of the wing. The SR-71's rear fuselage protruded several feet providing an easy visual reference. (Lockheed)

completely impervious to JP-7 while remaining elastic enough to expand and contract sufficiently. Luckily, the JP-7 used by the Blackbirds had a high vapor point, and proved to be basically non-flammable when spilled on the ground (there are videos of lighted matches being tossed onto spilled JP-7 without causing ignition, although this was not a recommended procedure).

On 25 April 1962 Lockheed test pilot Louis Schalk took the A-12 for an unofficial first flight, flying less than two miles at an altitude of about 20 feet. This "flight" revealed that several control linkages were improperly connected. These were promptly repaired and on 26 April Schalk made a 40-minute maiden flight. Kelly Johnson noted that this "... was obviously a day for the A-12, in that $2 \times 6 = 12$." Regardless, immediately after take-off the aircraft began shedding the triangular fillets that covered the chines along the aircraft's nose. The fillets had to be recovered and reaffixed with a different, presumably stronger, epoxy cement, a process that took the next four days.

OXCART's "official" first flight took place on 30 April 1962, witnessed by a number of CIA and Air Force representatives. With Schalk again at the controls, the OXCART took-off at 170 knots and climbed to 30,000 feet, achieving a top speed of 340 knots during the 59 minute

In early 1963 Jim Eastham was confident enough in the handling of the A-12 to attempt an aerial refueling with a modified KC-135A (they had not become Q models yet). This KC-135 was based at Groom Lake later in the test program and used exclusively for refueling OXCART during the flight test series. (Lockheed)

All of the OXCART aircraft were capable of aerial refueling, including the two-seat "Titanium Goose" shown here. The Goose had a second cockpit installed over the "Q" bay to allow its use as a trainer. This aircraft was never re-engined with J58 engines, spending it entire career powered by J75s, which limited it to approximately Mach 1.6 and 40,000 feet. Otherwise it was identical to single-seat A-12s. (Lockheed)

flight. On 2 May 1962, during the second test flight, OXCART broke the sound barrier, achieving a speed of Mach 1.1.

Four more aircraft, including a two-seat trainer, arrived at Groom Lake before the end of 1962. Initial testing could not explore the A-12's maximum potential, since the J58 engines were still not ready. Developing this power plant to OXCART specifications proved much more difficult than had been expected because the J58 had to reach performance levels never before achieved by a jet engine. To simulate the environmental conditions that the J58 would endure during maximum power flight (Mach 3.2 at 97,000 feet), the power plant was tested in the exhaust stream of a J75 engine. In the course of this extremely severe testing, the J58's problems were gradually overcome. By January 1963 ten J58 engines had been delivered to Groom Lake, and the first flight with two J58 engines took place on 15 January 1963. Already delivered test aircraft were retrofitted with J58s, and all new aircraft were fitted with the larger powerplant at the factory. The one exception was the two-seat trainer, which was never retrofitted and carried the J75 engines throughout its career

An aerial view of the Lockheed facility at Plant 42, Site 2 in Palmdale, California. This was the location of most Blackbird heavy maintenance and modifications in the later years of the program. Visible here are the nine surviving OXCART aircraft after they were placed in storage. For years it was possible to drive up to the gate at the edge of the facility and look at the Blackbirds. Later, however, a gate was installed at the public end of the access road which restricted visitors to official business only. (Lockheed)

The period devoted to OXCART flight tests was remarkably short considering the performance envelope which was being opened. By the end of 1963 there had been 573 flights totaling 765 hours by the nine aircraft in the inventory. On 20 July 1963 an A-12 first flew at Mach 3 and in November 1963 the design speed of Mach 3.2 was reached at 78,000 feet altitude. The longest sustained flight at design conditions occurred on 3 February 1964, lasting ten minutes at Mach 3.2 and 83,000 feet. By the end of 1964 there had been 1,160 flights, totaling 1,616 hours, with nine hours above Mach 3. Eleven aircraft were then available, four of them reserved for testing and seven assigned to the operational detachment.

By 20 November 1965 the final vali-

The only two-seat A-12 was the "Titanium Goose" (60-6927) which some reports have referred to as the A-12B. This was the only Blackbird that Kelly Johnson ever flew in. This aircraft spent its entire career powered by J75 engines and in the natural metal paint scheme. Noteworthy in this photograph are the metal vertical stabilizers (natural metal finish instead of the black finish of the composite units). (Lockheed via Tony Landis)

The second A-12 (60-6925) forward fuselage under construction at Burbank. The simple jigs and crowded conditions are noteworthy. This was easily the largest manufacturing program ever undertaken by Skunk Works at the time, and severely taxed their facilities. (Lockheed)

dation flights prior to OXCART deployment were completed. During these tests, an A-12 achieved a maximum speed of Mach 3.29 at 90,000 feet, and sustained flight above Mach 3.2 for 74 minutes. On 22 November, Kelly Johnson wrote to the CIA stating, "The time has come when the bird should leave its nest." Three years and seven months after its first flight, OXCART was ready for operational use. It was now time to find work for the most advanced aircraft ever conceived and built.

Although OXCART had been designed to replace the U-2 as a strategic reconnaissance aircraft to overfly the Soviet Union, this use had become doubtful long before the A-12 was ready for operational use. The Powers U-2 incident in 1960 made the United States very reluctant to consider overflights of the Soviet Union. Indeed, Presidents Eisenhower and Kennedy both stated publicly that the United States would not conduct such overflights. There was, however, a great deal of interest in deploying the aircraft to Southeast Asia, where US military activity was increasing. On 18 March 1965, the CIA and DoD agreed to go ahead with all the preparatory steps needed for the OXCART to operate over Vietnam.

Project BLACK SHIELD called for A-12s to be based at Kadena AB on Okinawa where $3.7 million was spent during 1965 to provide support facilities and secure real-time communications. During the first half of 1966, the CIA raised the issue of deploying OXCART to Okinawa five separate times but failed to win support from the White House.

When they were first removed from service, the OXCART aircraft were stored indoors at Palmdale. They were moved outside when the facility was needed to conduct heavy maintenance and modifications to the SR-71 fleet. By this time the entire OXCART fleet had been painted in overall black, with the exception of the two-seat "Titanium Goose" trainer located at the back of the this photo. The very last aircraft visible was the only surviving M-21. (Lockheed)

In May 1967 it was suggested that OXCART be used to determine whether surface-to-air missiles had been introduced undetected into North Vietnam, and this was approved by President Johnson on 16 May. The airlift of personnel and equipment to Kadena began on 17

May 1967, and on 22 May an A-12 (60-6937) flew nonstop from Groom Lake to Kadena in six hours and six minutes. By 29 May 1967, just 13 days after President Johnson's approval, BLACK SHIELD was ready to fly an operational mission.

On 31 May 1967 the first BLACK SHIELD mission flew one pass over North Vietnam and another over the demilitarized zone (DMZ). The mission was flown at Mach 3.1 and 80,000 feet, lasted three hours and 39 minutes, and photographed 70 of the 190 suspected surface-to-air sites and nine other priority targets. The A-12's ECM equipment did not detect any radar signals during the mission, which indicated that the flight had gone completely unnoticed by both the Chinese and North Vietnamese. During the next six weeks, there were seven more BLACK SHIELD missions.

Between 16 August and 31 December 1967 there were fifteen additional BLACK SHIELD missions. On 17 December one SAM site tracked an A-12 with its acquisition radar but was unsuccessful with its FAN SONG guidance radar. On 28 October 1967 a North Vietnamese SAM site launched a single missile at OXCART. Photography from this mission showed exhaust smoke above the SAM firing site, and pictures of the missile and of its contrail as it fell harmlessly back to Earth.

The only time the North Vietnamese came close to downing an OXCART was on 30 October 1967 when at least six missiles were fired at an A-12, each confirmed by vapor trails on mission photography. The pilot saw these vapor trails and witnessed three missile detonations behind the A-12, which was traveling at Mach 3.1 at 84,000 feet.

Post-flight inspection of the aircraft revealed that a piece of metal had penetrated the lower right wing fillet area and lodged against the support structure of the wing tank. The fragment was not a warhead pellet but may have been a part of the debris from one of the missile detonations.

Four BLACK SHIELD missions were flown during the first three months of 1968, with the last overflight of Vietnam taking place on 8 March 1968. During this same three-month period, the OXCART made its first overflight of North Korea after the USS Pueblo was seized on 23 January 1968.

Secretary of State Dean Rusk was reluctant to endorse a second mission over North Korea for fear of diplomatic repercussions should the aircraft come down in hostile territory. The Secretary was assured that the aircraft could transit North Korea in seven minutes, and the mission was finally flown on 19 February. The third and last overflight of North Korea occurred on 8 May 1968, and also proved to be the last operational OXCART mission.

Almost a decade had elapsed between the time when the concept for the OXCART aircraft was first examined and the first A-12 operationally deployed. Then after only 29 operational missions, the most advanced aircraft ever built was retired. The abandonment of the OXCART did not result from any shortcomings of the aircraft, but lay in fiscal pressures and competition between the reconnaissance programs of the CIA and the Air Force.

The 12 single-seat A-12s accumulated slightly over 3,727 hours of flight time during 2,189 flights. The lone two-seat trainer added another 1,076 hours in 614 flights. Of the 13 A-12s, five single-seat A-12 aircraft were lost in accidents during the OXCART program, and the eight remaining aircraft were retired to non-flyable storage at Plant 42 in Palmdale. No OXCARTs were lost to enemy action.

A line of OXCARTs being assembled. The size of the "Q" bay opening behind the cockpit on the closest aircraft is noteworthy. (Lockheed)

ADVANCED MANNED INTERCEPTOR

BLACKBIRDS TO DEFEND THE AMERICAS

Early during the development of OXCART, Kelly Johnson investigated the possibility of converting the aircraft into a bomber. The initial concept studied by Lockheed involved carrying simple unguided gravity "special"

(nuclear) bombs. These bombs were the result of breakthroughs in miniaturizing nuclear warheads for the Polaris submarine-launched ballistic missile. Four 400-pound bombs could be carried on a rotary rack located in the same Q-bay that

normally housed the camera equipment. Depending on the exact length of the weapons, the #1 fuel tank might have to be shortened somewhat to make room. No external changes were envisioned except for the necessary bomb-bay doors on the underside of the fuselage, and the full radar attenuation features of the A-12 would be retained. A small force of these high-speed bombers would provide a powerful deterrent since it was highly unlikely they would be detected on the way to their targets, and even more unlikely that they could be intercepted.

A forward fuselage mockup was reviewed by Gen. Curtis LeMay on 5 July 1961 who expressed considerable interest and asked if it could be adapted to carry air-to-surface missiles and associated guidance equipment. Johnson responded favorably, noting that to achieve the requested 200-foot CEP this was preferable to the gravity bomb solution. But although LeMay was interested in the possibilities, he indicated to Johnson that it was unlikely that the bomber version would be approved. The primary rationale was not technical, but rather that the Blackbird could be perceived as a threat to SAC's high-

The YF-12As were constructed in a cordoned-off section of Building 309/310 in Burbank since they were being built under a different security arrangement than the CIA's OXCART aircraft. Noteworthy in this view is the AN/ASG-18 radar and the location of the second seat. (Lockheed)

est priority project, the North American B-70 Valkyrie. Even so, as late as a 26 October 1961 memo from the Air Force to Lockheed, there was still a possibility that a bomber version could have been ordered. But no order for a strike version of the Blackbird ever materialized.

Always looking for new opportunities, Kelly Johnson had periodically proposed a high-speed interceptor based on the A-12 design to the Air Force. Internally, the interceptor was referred to as the AF-12 and in late October 1960 the Air Force awarded a $1 million contract to Lockheed under project KEDLOCK. Lockheed's vision, not necessarily shared by the Air Force, was that a fleet of 93 high-speed interceptors could adequately protect the North American continent against most expected Soviet threats from directions other than those expected (and well defended) over the North Pole.

As originally conceived by Kelly Johnson's engineering team the AF-12 was an A-12 modified with the AN/ASG-18 fire control system from the still-born North American XF-108 Rapier and three GAR-9 radar-guided air-to-air missiles. The pilot's seat was raised for better visibility and a second seat (for the radar officer) added in a deeper forward fuselage. This bulged canopy area gave the AF-12 a distinctive appearance amongst the Blackbirds.

The first YF-12A (60-6934) in final assembly during early 1963. The missing skin panels on the outer wing surface allowed access to the multitude of control cables and hydraulic lines that operated the outboard elevons. The YF-12As were usually fitted with metal vertical stabilizers during their entire career since defeating radar was not a primary concern for the interceptor variant. (Lockheed)

In order to minimize distortion of the radar signals, the aerodynamic chines on the extreme nose had to be deleted and the radome lengthened, although the aircraft was slightly shorter overall. The modified chines accommodated a pair of infrared search and track (IRST) sensors, generally similar to the ones used on the F-101 and F-102 interceptors. The aft fuselage, wings, nacelles, and engines were identical to the CIA's A-12.

By early 1961 a mockup of the forward fuselage had been constructed and on 31 May 1961 it was inspected by an Air Force group

Hughes used a modified Convair B-58 Hustler (55-665) named "Snoopy" to test the AN/ASG-18 and GAR-9 weapons systems. The nose of the B-58 was substantially modified to accommodate the large diameter

of the ASG-18 radar dish. Two specially configured pods were manufactured by Convair to house a single GAR-9 missile and its associated support equipment. Upon completion of the ASG-18 test series, this B-58 was stricken from the inventory and moved onto the photo test range at Edwards where it has sat since. It is currently earmarked to be included in the Edwards Flight Test Museum if funds and parts can be found to restore it. (Tony Landis Collection)

The Hughes AN/ASG-18 pulse Doppler radar was the most powerful airborne radar in the world at the time of its development. This radar and its associated GAR-9 Super Falcon missile were originally developed for the North American XF-108 Rapier escort fighter prior to that aircraft's cancellation. Many of the technologies developed for the ASG-18 found their way into the production AN/AWG-9 radar used by the Navy F-14 Tomcat. (Lockheed)

that was generally very pleased with the progress being made. Unfortunately, by June 1961 wind tunnel tests revealed that the revised nose and cockpit configuration caused directional stability problems at high Mach. In an effort to solve this, a large folding ventral stabilizer was added under the aft fuselage, and a small fixed ventral fin was added under each engine nacelle. This gave the AF-12 a very distinctive in-flight appearance.

The Hughes AN/ASG-18 was the first coherent pulse-Doppler radar designed in the United States. It was capable of long-range (~100 mile) look-down or look-up operation, but could only track a single target at a time. The AN/ASG-18 system had been born in July 1956 when the Air Defense Command formulated specifications and characteristics that gave birth to the North American XF-108 Rapier. Hughes had subcontracted to develop the radar system, and when the Rapier program was cancelled, had joined forces with Lockheed to promote the development of an interceptor version of the A-12.

On 17 October 1958 Convair had received a contract to modify a single B-58A (55-665) and to manufacture two specially configured pods

The AIM-54 Phoenix (right) was developed largely from technology originally conceived for the GAR-9 (AIM-47) Super Falcon (left) used by the YF-12A. One of the largest differences was that the AIM-47 was scheduled to use a 250 kiloton nuclear warhead, while the AIM-54 uses a conventional warhead with a proximity fuse. The aerosurfaces also differ somewhat in order to improve the maneuverability of the AIM-54 which was designed to intercept cruise-missiles instead of supersonic bombers. (Hughes)

for AN/ASG-18 testing. The special pods were completed on 15 July 1959 and featured a large internal bay for a single GAR-9 missile, a freon cooling system, telemetry equipment, and tracking flares. Unlike normal B-58 pods they did not carry fuel. Two weeks later, on 2 August 1959, the B-58 modifications were completed and the aircraft delivered to Hughes who then installed the AN/ASG-18 fire control system, including its hydraulically actuated 40-inch antenna.

The B-58 was equipped with a nose radome that was seven feet longer than normal. Later in the test program an infrared sensor would be mounted on each side of the forward fuselage, approximating the relationship of the sensors and the radar antenna in the YF-12A installation. The IRST sensors initially operated in the 2.5 micron range, but this was modified several times as test results were analyzed. The second and third crew stations of the B-58 also received substantial modifications to accommodate the AN/ASG-18 displays and controls, and to delete the normal offensive and defensive systems.

Initial ground tests with the complete system included dummy GAR-9 launches into a styrofoam-

One of the YF-12As at Groom Lake before the IRST sensors had been added to the front of the chines. The drag chute doors are open on the top of the aft fuselage. The size of the perfectly circular radome is clearly evident in this photograph. (Lockheed)

lined pit, and additional dummy launches while the aircraft was airborne. The first flight of an ASG-18 system aboard the B-58 took place in early 1960. In August 1961 the first GAR-9 missile was ground-launched to verify the rocket engine's performance. By January 1962 three unguided ground-launches had been accomplished, and on 15 January a guided round came within 55 feet of its QF-80 drone target flying at 13,500 feet.

The GAR-9 Super Falcon missile presented its own problems. Nobody had ever attempted to launch a missile at Mach 3 before, and the XF-108 program had not gotten far enough along to work out the problems. Furthermore, no one seemed to be in agreement as to how to go about doing it. Several solutions existed on paper, and the wind tunnel had confirmed the basic philosophies, but it would take actual experimentation to prove the concepts.

The first YF-12A (60-6934) prepares for a flight at Groom Lake. Interestingly, at this point it appears that composite vertical stabilizers have been fitted. This photograph was taken fairly late in the test program at Groom Lake since the camera pods under the engine nacelles have been fitted. These were not added until the YF-12A's were ready to begin missile ejection trials. (Lockheed)

This was the normal configuration for the three YF-12As during their testing at Groom Lake. The natural metal finish shows the metal vertical stabilizers. Although the area immediately below the canopies was painted non-glare black, the canopies themselves were left natural metal, unlike the A-12s that usually received black canopies. Note the absence of the under-nacelle camera pods. (Lockheed)

On 25 May 1962 the first GAR-9 air-to-air launch was conducted from Snoopy while the aircraft was flying at 36,000 feet over the Edwards test range. The guided round passed within six feet of a QF-80 target drone that was approximately 15 miles distant from the B-58. A similar test on 17 August 1962 resulted in the missile grazing the side of the QF-80 target.

However, a guided launch on 21 February 1963 against a Vought Regulus II target resulted in the GAR-9 breaking up in-flight. Testing was halted while Hughes attempted to understand the failure. This opportunity was also used to improve the availability of the B-58 test bed which had been suffering severe maintenance difficulties. By July 1963 both the GAR-9 and the B-58 had been modified and additional flight tests scheduled.

The forward fuselage mock-up for the production F-12B. Extensive wind tunnel work, along with careful tuning of the ASG-18 computers, allowed Lockheed to include a partial chine on the radome, eliminating the large center folding ventral stabilizer. The smaller ventral stabilizers under the engine nacelles would have been retained by the F-12B, but eliminating the weight and hydraulic complexity of the central ventral was considered a major improvement. The IRST sensors were also better faired into the chines, eliminating some of the drag penalty they imposed on the YF-12As. (Lockheed)

The first YF-12A (60-6934) departs Edwards AFB on a test flight. Until the aircraft were turned over to NASA this was the standard configuration. All three aircraft were painted an overall black and usually carried the camera pods under the engine nacelles. An Air Force Systems Command badge was on the right vertical stabilizer, while an Air Defense Command badge was on the left. Noteworthy is that the main landing gear is half retracted before the nose gear even begins. (Lockheed)

WARBIRD**TECH**
S E R I E S

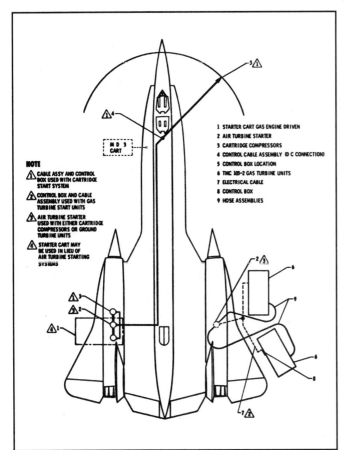

NOTE

⚠ CABLE ASSY AND CONTROL BOX USED WITH CARTRIDGE START SYSTEM

⚠ CONTROL BOX AND CABLE ASSEMBLY USED WITH GAS TURBINE START UNITS

⚠ AIR TURBINE STARTER USED WITH EITHER CARTRIDGE COMPRESSORS OR GROUND TURBINE UNITS

⚠ STARTER CART MAY BE USED IN LIEU OF AIR TURBINE STARTING SYSTEMS

1 STARTER CART GAS ENGINE DRIVEN
2 AIR TURBINE STARTER
3 CARTRIDGE COMPRESSORS
4 CONTROL CABLE ASSEMBLY (D C CONNECTION)
5 CONTROL BOX LOCATION
6 TMC 105-2 GAS TURBINE UNITS
7 ELECTRICAL CABLE
8 CONTROL BOX
9 HOSE ASSEMBLIES

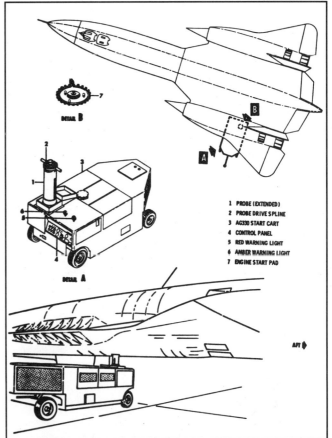

1 PROBE (EXTENDED)
2 PROBE DRIVE SPLINE
3 AG330 START CART
4 CONTROL PANEL
5 RED WARNING LIGHT
6 AMBER WARNING LIGHT
7 ENGINE START PAD

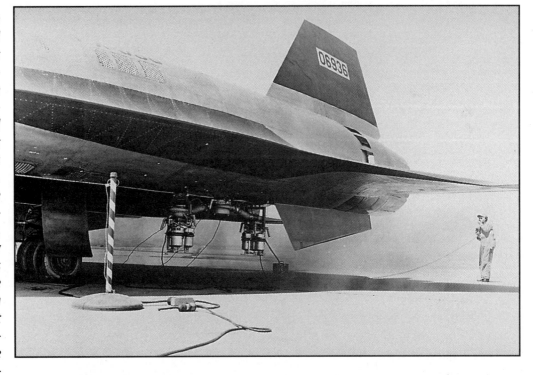

To meet an Air Force requirement for rapid response to intercept alerts, Lockheed developed two alternate starting systems in addition to the normal "Buick" starting cart used by the OXCARTs and later by the SR-71s. In the photograph, the center object is the normal vertical drive shaft, similar to that used by the "Buick" starting carts The object on either side of the drive shaft is a cartridge starter that used a chemical reaction to spin the drive shaft to speed. A turbine-powered starting cart was also developed. Both of these systems were deemed more compatible with the interceptor role, but both were more expensive to purchase and maintain and were not used extensively by the Blackbirds. Noteworthy in the drawing that shows the normal "Buick" cart system (upper right) is the fact that the drawing clearly shows an SR-71, even though the illustration is from a YF-12A manual. (Lockheed)

Hughes completed the first AN/ASG-18 system for the YF-12A in late 1961, and in early 1962 it was installed on 60-6934. By late 1963 the YF-12As were capable of conducting fully guided launches of the GAR-9, and the use of the B-58 test bed began to decline. The last launches from "Snoopy" occurred in February 1964, and the aircraft was retired shortly thereafter. All the ASG-18 equipment was removed from the B-58 to support the YF-12A test program, and the B-58 airframe was moved to the Edwards AFB photo range.

The ASG-18 employed a liquid-cooled transmitter train consisting of two traveling wave tube amplifiers in tandem to provide the desired gain, and analog circuitry for the generation and processing of the coherent high pulse repetition frequency wave form. The radar consisted of 41 separate units weighing nearly 1,400 pounds that occupied most of the nose, plus the equipment bay that would logically have contained the fourth GAR-9 missile. The entire package included a solid-state digital computer for navigation and firing solutions; an analog attack steering computer; and an infrared search and track system capable of being slaved to the radar.

From a top view the cut-off chines of the third YF-12A (60-6936) show up well. By this time in its flight test program the IRST sensors had been removed. Large red walkways were painted on the top wing surface of most Blackbirds. The refueling receptacle is open here, and soon the interceptor will begin to take on fuel from the KC-135Q tanker. (Lockheed)

A Lockheed family portrait at Edwards AFB in the early 1960s. From the rear: C-141 Starlifter, HC-130 Hercules, T-33 Shooting Star; U-2A, F-104A Starfighter, and a YF-12A. Except for the two transports, all of these designs originated within the fertile mind of Kelly Johnson and Skunk Works, and even the C-130 was developed using "Skunk Works methods." (Lockheed)

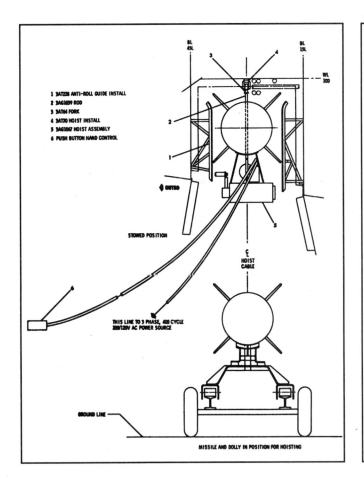

1 3AT228 ANTI-ROLL GUIDE INSTALL
2 3AG1209 ROD
3 3A764 FORK
4 3AT70 HOIST INSTALL
5 3AG1067 HOIST ASSEMBLY
6 PUSH BUTTON HAND CONTROL

STOWED POSITION

HOIST CABLE

THIS LINE TO 3 PHASE, 400 CYCLE 208/120V AC POWER SOURCE

GROUND LINE

MISSILE AND DOLLY IN POSITION FOR HOISTING

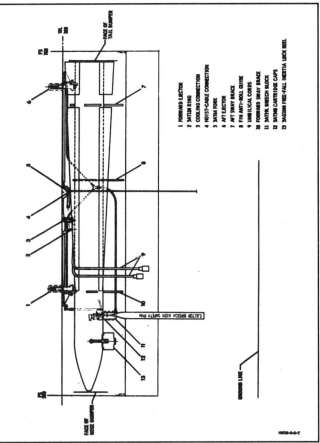

1 FORWARD EJECTOR
2 3AT23M RING
3 COOLING CONNECTION
4 HOIST-CABLE CONNECTION
5 3ATM FORK
6 AFT EJECTOR
7 AFT SWAY BRACE
8 FIN ANTI-ROLL GUIDE
9 UMBILICAL CORDS
10 FORWARD SWAY BRACE
11 3ATVL BREECH BLOCK
12 3AT248 CARTRIDGE CAPS
13 3AG20M FREE-FALL INERTIA LOCK REEL

FACE OF TAIL BUMPER

EJECTOR BREECH ASSY SAFETY PIN

GROUND LINE

FACE OF NOSE BUMPER

The YF-12As carried three GAR-9 (AIM-47) air-to-air missiles in separate weapons bays under the forward fuselage. The missiles were transported on special carts that were towed by a standard USAF ramp tug and placed under an open weapons bay. Once positioned under the YF-12A the missiles were hoisted into position using power winches. Special care had to be taken with operational weapons since they would have been equipped with nuclear warheads. (US Air Force)

The ASG-18 provided Hughes with much of the technology later used to design the Navy's AN/AWG-9 system successfully employed in the Grumman F-14 Tomcat. The GAR-9 missile, later redesignated AIM-47, would form the basis for the AIM-54 Phoenix.

The second YF-12A being escorted by a NASA/Lockheed F-104 Starfighter soon after NASA began flying the Blackbirds. A little later in the test program NASA painted the characteristic yellow NASA banner across the Blackbird's vertical stabilizers and deleted the two Air Force command badges. The large central ventral fin is in the full down position. The resemblance between the F-104's ventral fin and the ones under the engine nacelles on the Blackbird is very evident here. (Lockheed)

VIPs watch a YF-12A streak by on its way to setting several world's records at Edwards AFB on 1 May 1965. The first YF-12A (60-6934) set a sustained altitude record of 80,257.65 feet with Col. Robert Stephens and LtCol. Daniel Andre and also a 15/25 kilometer closed course record of 2,070.101 mph with the same crew. The third YF-12A (60-6936) set a 500 kilometer closed course record of 1,643.042 mph with Maj. Walter Daniel and Maj. Noel Warner. On a separate flight, 60-6936 also set three 1,000 kilometer closed course (without payload, with 1,000 kilogram payload, and with 2,000 kilogram payload) records of 1,688.891 mph with Maj Walter Daniel and Capt. James Cooney. (Lockheed)

A retouched photo of the first YF-12A (60-6934) at Groom Lake. Most of the early photographs were retouched to disguise the mountains in the background that easily identified the facility as Groom Lake. Unfortunately, most of the originals have been lost along the way, leaving only the retouched versions. Here the aircraft is getting ready for ground testing of its ASG-18 radar set, evidenced by the large rack of test equipment below the cockpit area, and the multitude of signs warning of radiation hazards. (Lockheed via Tony Landis)

The Air Force finally ordered three AF-12s and negotiated with the CIA to use the seventh, eighth, and ninth A-12 airframes to speed the project along. Due to security regulations (need-to-know), the AF-12 assembly area was separated from the normal A-12 production line by erecting walls around one corner of the Burbank facility. By August 1962 the major elements of the first AF-12 were in the assembly jigs. These same security concerns (Air Force crews need not know about the CIA spy program) also suggested that the AF-12 flight test program should be conducted somewhere besides Groom Lake, but in the end it was decided that economic and practical considerations outweighed security and the AF-12s would be tested at Groom Lake, at least initially.

The first AF-12 was trucked to Groom Lake in July 1963, and on 7 August Lockheed test pilot Jim Eastham made the aircraft's first flight. On 29 February 1964 part of the Blackbird's security blanket was removed when President Johnson announced, "The United States has successfully developed an advanced experimental jet aircraft, the A-11, which has been tested in sustained flight at more than 2,000 miles per hour and at altitudes in excess of 70,000 feet.

"The performance of the A-11 far exceeds that of any other aircraft in the world today. The development of this aircraft has been made possible by major advances in aircraft technology of great significance to both military and commercial application. Several A-11 aircraft are now being flight tested at Edwards AFB in California ... The A-11 aircraft now at Edwards AFB are undergoing extensive tests to

determine their capabilities as long-range interceptors." At the same time a proper Air Force designation (YF-12A) was assigned.

Of course this statement contained two non-truths. First, the reference to the A-11 was at Kelly Johnson's suggestion to mislead intelligence sources. Second, there were no Blackbirds of any description at Edwards AFB. Caught slightly off-guard by the President's announcement, two of the three YF-12As were hurriedly flown from Groom Lake to Edwards. In their haste to conceal the aircraft from public view, Lou Schalk and Jim Eastham made a direct approach and landing on Edwards runway, taxied directly to the awaiting hangers, were pushed in tail first, and the doors closed. The two YF-12As were still very hot from their dash from Groom Lake, and the heat set off the hanger's fire deluge system, covering the aircraft and ground crew in water.

Flight tests continued with increased frequency since they could be conducted without as many security restrictions. On 16 April 1964 the first XAIM-47 inert verification shape was ejected from a YF-12A in-flight. The launch was generally successful in that the missile separated cleanly from the aircraft, but its ejection angle left a great deal to be desired. If the missile had been powered, it would have immediately flown through

The main gear has just touched down but the braking parachute has not been deployed yet. Like most delta-wing aircraft the YF-12A landed nose-high, creating some visibility problems for the pilot who could not see around the aircraft's chines. (NASA via Tony Landis)

For most of their time in NASA service the three YF-12As had a yellow NASA logo on their vertical stabilizers. Noteworthy is the "buzz number" on the engine intake has been shortened from "FX-935" to simply "935." Large specially designed access stands were used for crew access to avoid damage to the composite chine panels. (NASA via Tony Landis)

The COLD WALL experiment was mounted on the bottom of the second YF-12A (60-6935). Since the experiment was mounted in roughly the same location as one of the AIM-47 missile bays, it was an easy task to adapt the camera pods to photograph it in flight. The large central ventral fin unique to the YF-12As shows up well here. (NASA via Tony Landis)

The COLD WALL, a Langley-supported heat-transfer experiment, consisted of a stainless steel tube equipped with thermocouples and pressure-sensing equipment. A special insulation coating covered the liquid nitrogen-chilled tube for the first part of the flight. At Mach 3 the insulation could be pyrotechnically blown away from the tube, instantly exposing it to the thermal environment. This data could be compared with results taken from testing a similar tube using ground-based wind-tunnel facilities and would validate ground research methods. (NASA via Tony Landis)

Late in its flight test program with NASA the large central ventral fin was deleted from the YF-12A. It was found that the loss of the fin did not seriously affect the aircraft's stability, and that Lockheed engineers had been overly conservative when they originally designed the aircraft. A small fin with various air-test transducers has been mounted at the location normally used by the fin so that it could take advantage of the folding mechanism. (NASA via Tony Landis)

the YF-12's cockpit. Obviously more work was needed.

On 9 January 1965 Jim Eastham reached Mach 3.23 with the first YF-12A, and sustained Mach 3.2 for over five minutes. Work on the ASG-18 and AIM-47 proceeded slowly, but on 18 March 1965 one of the YF-12A's launched a single YAIM-47 and hit a drone flying 36 miles away with a closure rate of over 2,000 MPH.

The various Blackbirds had routinely broken just about every speed record in existence, but nobody knew due to the security restrictions surrounding the programs. On 12 August 1964 the Air Force asked Lockheed to come up with a program to use one of the YF-12As to publicly break the records. The YF-12A was chosen primarily because it was the model with the greatest public exposure and was also the one with the least design and technology sensitivity. Not to mention it was easier to explain why the Air Force needed such a high-speed aircraft while it was more difficult to explain the CIA's need, or indeed, why the CIA even had an air force.

The program languished for some time, but finally on 1 May 1965 the first and third YF-12As were used to set several Class C Group III absolute records, including: sustained altitude – 80,257.65 feet (Col. Robert Stephens and LtCol. Daniel Andre); 15/25 kilometer closed course – 2,070.101 MPH (Col. Robert Stephens and LtCol. Daniel Andre); 500 kilometer closed course – 1,643.042 MPH (Maj. Walter Daniel and Maj. Noel Warner); and three 1,000 kilometer closed course (without payload, with 1,000 kilogram payload, and with 2,000 kilo-

gram payload) – 1,688.891 MPH (Maj Walter Daniel and Capt. James Cooney).

The YF-12 program took a step closer to production on 14 May 1965 when the Air Force funded a $500,000 contract for engineering development of the follow-on F-12B. This would have been the operational configuration of the YF-12A, and would be designed to be deployed without the need for the extensive ground systems required of the A-12 and YF-12A prototypes. An additional $500,000 was released to Lockheed on 10 November 1965 for continued engineering work on the F-12B. At the same time, $4.5 million was issued to Hughes for continued development of the ASG-18 fire control system. Externally the F-12B would more closely resemble the A-12 than the YF-12A. Careful shaping of the radome allowed the addition of small chines, improving the aerodynamics and eliminating the need for the large central ventral fins. Although the aircraft would still not be quite as stable as the basic A-12, engineers felt the instability would be well within the ability of the stability augmentation system to damp out. Besides, the F-12 probably did not need to be absolutely as stable as the photo-reconnaissance A-12.

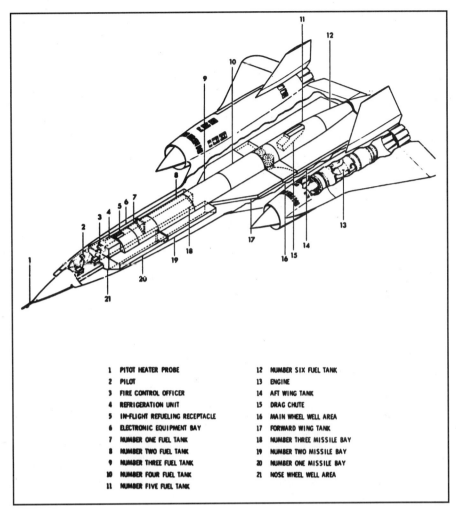

1	PITOT HEATER PROBE	12	NUMBER SIX FUEL TANK
2	PILOT	13	ENGINE
3	FIRE CONTROL OFFICER	14	AFT WING TANK
4	REFRIGERATION UNIT	15	DRAG CHUTE
5	IN-FLIGHT REFUELING RECEPTACLE	16	MAIN WHEEL WELL AREA
6	ELECTRONIC EQUIPMENT BAY	17	FORWARD WING TANK
7	NUMBER ONE FUEL TANK	18	NUMBER THREE MISSILE BAY
8	NUMBER TWO FUEL TANK	19	NUMBER TWO MISSILE BAY
9	NUMBER THREE FUEL TANK	20	NUMBER ONE MISSILE BAY
10	NUMBER FOUR FUEL TANK	21	NOSE WHEEL WELL AREA
11	NUMBER FIVE FUEL TANK		

In reality there were four bays on the YF-12A, but the right forward bay was occupied by the electronics necessary for the ASG-18 radar and its fire control system. The other three bays housed GAR-9 (AIM-47) missiles. Like the other Blackbirds, the majority of the YF-12A's fuselage was given over to fuel tanks, broken only by space for the main landing gear and drag chute compartments. (US Air Force)

Eventually researchers did get a successful test of the COLD WALL, but the experiment caused numerous in-flight difficulties. On the last COLD WALL flight, for example, the YF-12A (60-6935) experienced a simultaneous dual unstart followed by rough engine operation after firing the COLD WALL. As it descended, anxiously followed by the YF-12C (60-6937,

a.k.a. SR-71A 64-19751) photo-chase, the latter aircraft also experienced multiple unstarts. Both aircraft limped back to Edwards at reduced power and NASA grounded them for extended inspections. (NASA via Tony Landis)

A bottom view of the number two YF-12A (60-6935) shows the COLD WALL experiment after its protective cover had been jettisoned. The large camera pods under the engine nacelles housed a variety of still and motion cameras, including a very high-speed camera to provide accurate engineering data on events taking place under the aircraft (missile drops or the COLD WALL). (NASA via Tony Landis)

On 28 September 1965, an AIM-47 was fired from a YF-12A at Mach 3.2 flying at 75,000 feet. Telemetry showed that the missile missed its intended target, flying 36 miles away at 40,000 feet, by less than seven feet. The Air Force was ready to test the ASG-18 against realistic targets in hard to detect and track environments. On 25 April 1966, the first and third aircraft were flown to Eglin AFB, Florida, for firing trials. The same day, Jim Eastham in the first YF-12A fired an unarmed AIM-47 against a QB-47 flying 60,000 feet below the Blackbird (which was flying at 75,000 feet and Mach 3.2). The missile passed through the QB-47's horizontal stabilizer. If the missile had been armed, the bomber would have been destroyed. Altogether, the

YF-12's weapons system scored an impressive six hits out of seven attempts. The single miss was attributed to a defective missile gyro system.

But it was all not to be. Although Lockheed had recommended taking the program to Holloman AFB, New Mexico, to fire against targets flying in the desert ground clutter, the Air Force had run out of money, and ordered the YF-12s placed into storage at Edwards AFB. By August 1967, Lockheed had laid off or reassigned over half of the F-12 test team, retaining just enough personnel to put the aircraft into storage and clean up the documentation. By Christmas the Air Force had decided not to pursue the F-12B follow-on program.

On 5 January 1968 a formal order was issued that shut down the F-12B program in its entirety. A similar order for the YF-12A program followed on 1 February 1968. The cancellation notice on the YF-12A program included orders to destroy all tooling for both the fighter and reconnaissance (SR-71) variants. To comply with this order, the large assembly jigs were cut up and sold to local scrap dealers for seven cents per pound. However, many smaller tools and fixtures were placed in storage at nearby Norton

For its record breaking flights the third YF-12A (60-6936) had a large white cross painted on its belly as a photographic reference. The three white silhouettes on the nose were painted after the record flights to commemorate the event. The small ribbon above the serial number on the vertical stabilizer is a Presidential Unit Citation. Noteworthy is the length of the tow bar necessary to clear the long nose on the Blackbird. (NASA via Tony Landis)

AFB, and supported the manufacture of spare parts for the SR-71s for many years. After the cancellation of the F-12B program the YF-12As were placed into flyable storage.

YF-12s WITH NASA

NASA's involvement with the Blackbird began in earnest during 1967. NASA wanted an instrumented SR-71A to use for its own research, but failing that, NASA was willing to install an instrument package on one of the SR-71A test aircraft. The Air Force declined, but offered NASA the use of two YF-12As (60-6935 and 6936) then in storage at Edwards. A team from the Air Defense Command would be made available for maintenance and logistics support. A memorandum of understanding was signed 5 June 1969 followed by a public announcement on 18 July.

NASA and Air Force technicians spent three months getting the YF-12A (60-6935) ready for flight and the joint flight research program got under way with a successful maiden flight on 10 December 1969. Flight Research Center (FRC) and Langley engineers were very interested in measuring flight loads, which vary depending on aerodynamic conditions and the effects of structural heating. At some future date, engineers planned to move the aircraft into the High Temperature Loads Laboratory, heat it, and determine how much of the measured flight loads stemmed from structural heating. When an airframe is heated, the induced thermal stresses change the shape of the structure even without loads being applied. The changed airframe shape then has a much different load distribution pattern. To predict loads and struc-

No in-flight photographs exist of this particular modification to one of the YF-12As, and no record of it having flown in this configuration has been found. But several detail photos showing this canard installation have been located. NASA was extremely interested in the altitude-holding capability of an eventual supersonic transport (SST) and it is possible that this experiment was intended to investigate pitch control laws. (NASA via Tony Landis)

Returning home from a test flight, the number two YF-12A (60-6935) appears as if it could be returning from a successful intercept mission. The center ventral fin proved to be mostly unnecessary and would have been deleted from any production F-12B model. (Tony Landis Collection)

The Blackbird series was based on a large double-delta planform with blended chines on the forward fuselage and outboard on the engine nacelles. A fuel dump was located in the extreme rear fuselage, which provided one of the most readily apparent visible clues to differentiate the SR-71 from earlier Blackbirds. Here one of the YF-12As shows the standard A-12/F-12 rear fuselage configuration, with the fuel dump basically even with the trailing edge of the wing. On the SR-71 the rear fuselage was extended several feet aft of the trailing edge. The cut-off nose chines unique to the YF-12As show up well from this angle. (NASA via Tony Landis)

The other YF-12A (60-6936) had just embarked on its joint NASA-Air Force research program when it crashed. During a flight 24 June 1971 the Blackbird experienced fatigue failure of a fuel line, resulting in a fire in the right engine nacelle. LtCol. Ronald J. Layton and Maj. Billy A. Curtis debated whether they could land the burning Blackbird but they wisely elected to eject. The YF-12A crashed n the desert near Edward's runway and the remains were later moved to a commercial scrap yard in nearby Rosamond.

NASA had wanted to add a third aircraft to the YF-12A test program

tural response, NASA developed two computer modeling programs using a technique known as finite element analysis, and one of the major objectives of the flight test program was to compare the actual results with the predicted data. NASA also installed a Hasselblad camera within the YF-12A's fuselage to photograph the deformation of the structure and found that under certain conditions the aircraft experienced as much as 0.6 inches of deflection at the aft end of the fuselage.

One of a variety of photo reference markings used by the YF-12As (60-6935 here) during their career with NASA. The interceptor's cockpit was raised higher than the A-12 or SR-71 to provide additional visibility for the pilot, although it was still poor by fighter standards. (NASA via Tony Landis)

solely for propulsion tests. A month after the loss of 60-6936, the Air Force made the second SR-71 (64-17951) available to NASA. Because the SR-71 program was still shrouded in secrecy this aircraft was fictitiously designated YF-12C and carried the equally fictitious serial number 60-6937 (confusingly, this serial number was also used by an A-12). On 24 May 1972 the YF-12C made its first NASA flight.

By this time, NASA had already accumulated 53 flights in the YF-12A and was ready to place the aircraft in FRC's High Temperature Loads Laboratory. It remained in the lab for over a year, not flying again until July 1973. As a result of the correlation between flight tests and tests in the heat laboratory, FRC engineers were confident that they had developed simulations and instrumentation that would allow the aircraft industry to confidently proceed with the development of other high-temperature aircraft.

NASA approached the propulsion program on the YF-12C with a similar purpose in mind. Together with

Like all the Blackbirds, the YF-12As were transported out of Burbank in specially-built trailers. These were as large as allowed by law, and required a Highway Patrol escort during some parts of the journey. Exactly what Lockheed told the CHP was in the trailers is open for speculation! (Lockheed)

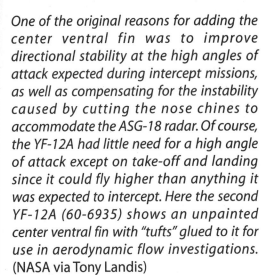

One of the original reasons for adding the center ventral fin was to improve directional stability at the high angles of attack expected during intercept missions, as well as compensating for the instability caused by cutting the nose chines to accommodate the ASG-18 radar. Of course, the YF-12A had little need for a high angle of attack except on take-off and landing since it could fly higher than anything it was expected to intercept. Here the second YF-12A (60-6935) shows an unpainted center ventral fin with "tufts" glued to it for use in aerodynamic flow investigations. (NASA via Tony Landis)

NASA engineers were interested in measuring flight loads which depended on the actual aerodynamic load conditions and the effects of structural heating. NASA moved the aircraft into the High Temperature Loads Laboratory and heated it to determine how much of the load stemmed from thermal heating of the structure. This laboratory consisted of a set of heating elements that were shaped around the YF-12A's fuselage, which was heavily instrumented with thermocouples and strain gauges. This allowed engineers to heat the airframe to the same temperatures usually observed during high-speed flight while controlling the other environmental factors (loads, etc.) (NASA via Tony Landis)

Lockheed and Pratt & Whitney, FRC engineers developed a computer model of the engine and inlet system. In conjunction with the Ames, Langley, and Lewis research centers, the flight data from the aircraft were compared with data taken from tests of scale-model inlets. These studies were very detailed, examining such questions as what percentage of airflow through the inlet exited through bypass doors in the inlet and what percentage actually passed through the engine. One surprise was the discovery that a strong vortex, coming from the fuselage chines, streamed into the middle of the inlet.

The FRC team also examined the inlet "unstart" anomaly that had plagued the Blackbirds throughout their careers. If the airflow was not properly matched to the engine, internal pressure would force the standing shock wave from inside to outside the inlet. This resulted in the loss of the thrust provided by inlet pressure recovery and the thrust imbalance generated a large yawing motion, as well as residual pitching and rolling tendencies. This

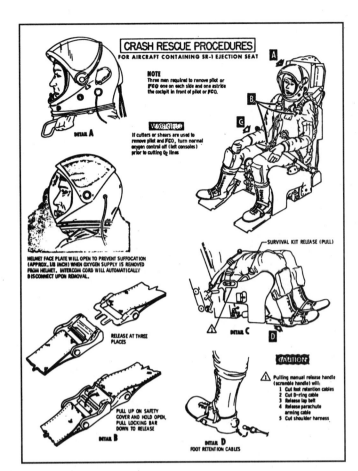

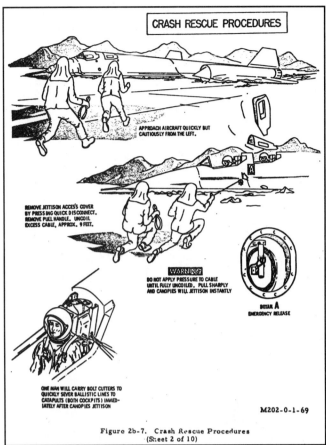

Figure 2b-7. Crash Rescue Procedures
(Sheet 2 of 10)

The Blackbirds presented a significant difference in ground rescue, primarily because of the use of full pressure suits by the pilots and the zero-zero ejection seats, something fairly new when the aircraft was introduced. There were also unusual hazards in the form of liquid nitrogen (LN2) and the triethylborane (TEB) igniter fluid used with the JP-7 fuel. The LN2 was housed in dewars in the nose wheel well. (US Air Force)

condition could not be tolerated on an SST aircraft and NASA devoted a great deal of energy to learn how to control unstarts, to the point of deliberately inducing them on test flights.

The NASA Blackbirds flew an average of once a week and program expenses averaged $3.1 million per year. The scope of what was

The upper wing surface with the skin removed. There was a great deal of structure inside the wing, contributing to the Blackbird's great strength. Small "standoffs" can be seen on each rib, providing attachment locations for the corrugated skin. (Tony Landis Collection)

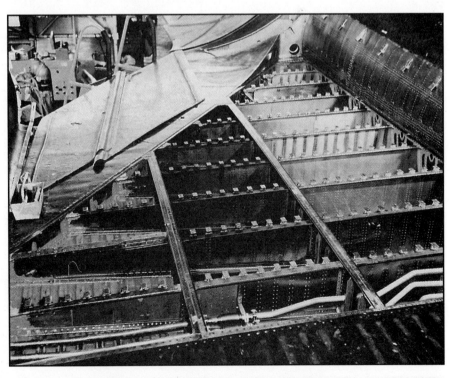

involved in a YF-12 flight was enormous. The Blackbird crew would suit up 1.5 hours before take-off, drive out to the flight line, and enter the aircraft. Other FRC personnel would ready an F-104 and T-38 to chase the Blackbird through Mach 2. The Air Force would send a KC-135Q tanker with a load of JP-7 from the SR-71 base at Beale AFB. After take-off the YF-12A would refuel from the tanker, accelerate to approximately Mach 0.9, dive (the most efficient way to exceed Mach 1), nose upward, and accelerate to the maximum speed selected for the flight, outrunning and out-ranging the chase aircraft. After one large circuit over the western United States, the Blackbird would decelerate and descend, take on more fuel from

The Hughes GAR-9 (AIM-47) air-to-air missile was 12.5 feet long, had a diameter of 13.5 inches, a fin span of 33 inches, and weighed over 800 pounds. Its maximum speed of Mach 4 was not significantly faster than the YF-12A that was launching it. It had an advertised maximum range in excess of 125 miles, although no intercepts were attempted at that distance. It was expected that production versions would use a 250 kiloton nuclear warhead. Much of the basic technology (minus the nuclear warhead) was later used to develop the AIM-54 Phoenix missile used by the F-111B and F-14. The YF-12As launched seven GAR-9s at speeds ranging from Mach 2.19 to Mach 3.2 – surprisingly six of these launches passed within lethal distance of their targets. (Lockheed)

NASA had little use for an interceptor, and the YF-12As were modified to carry research equipment in their missile bays. The size of electronic equipment during the 1970s is evident in these photos – similar equipment today would probably be less than half the size. The SR-71 is also capable of carrying equipment in bays located in approximately the same location as these. (Mick Roth)

Even at Edwards the weather does not always cooperate. The second YF-12A is being prepared for a test flight on a less than ideal day. The vapor at the lower right is from venting the liquid nitrogen dewars that are used to purge the fuel tanks as they are emptied. (Mick Roth)

the KC-135Q, again go supersonic, make another circuit, then return and land.

NASA's Blackbird program had its exciting moments, routine unstarts aside. On one YF-12C flight, Don Mallick and Ray Young experienced a stuck inlet spike, which caused the aircraft to burn prodigious amounts of fuel, necessitating an emergency landing at Fallon Naval Air Station, Nevada. Another time, during a stability test at Mach 0.9 with the aircraft's roll and yaw stability augmentation system deliberately turned off, they lost the folding ventral fin from NASA's YF-12A. The departing fin damaged the wing and aft fuselage, and ruptured a fuel tank. Fortunately this fin was needed only at high supersonic speeds and Mallick and Young skillfully brought the ailing Blackbird back to Edwards.

Tests of the Langley-developed COLD WALL experiment package offered some excitement as well. The COLD WALL consisted of a stainless steel tube equipped with thermocouples and pressure-sensing equipment. A special insulation covered the liquid nitrogen chilled tube during the first part of the flight. At Mach 3 the insulation could be pyrotechnically blown away from the tube, instantly exposing it to the thermal environment. This data could be compared with results taken from testing a

similar tube using ground-based wind-tunnel facilities to validate ground research methods. Eventually researchers did get a successful test, but the experiment caused numerous in-flight difficulties. For example, on the last COLD WALL flight the YF-12A experienced a dual simultaneous unstart followed by rough engine operation after firing the COLD WALL. As it descended the YF-12C photo-chase also experienced multiple unstarts. Both aircraft limped back to Edwards at reduced power and NASA grounded them for extended inspections.

Yes, the government does lie. While NASA flew this aircraft it was called a YF-12C, although there never was such an aircraft. The serial number on the tail (60-6937) was actually issued to an A-12, but not this aircraft. In reality this is the second SR-71 (64-17951) which was bailed to NASA after the third YF-12A was written off in a crash. There has been a great deal of speculation that this aircraft had modified intakes and engines to make it less sensitive, but this is unlikely, although all military reconnaissance and ECM equipment was deleted prior to its delivery to NASA. (Dennis R. Jenkins)

Flight tests of the YF-12s furnished some interesting data. For example, at Mach 3 fully 50% of the aircraft's total drag came from simply venting air overboard through the inlet bypass doors. Also, a gray area was discovered between stability and control. Inlet components

The Blackbird's main landing gear consisted of three wheels on each side, any one of which could support the aircraft at normal landing weights and were rated for a maximum speed of 239 knots. Each main gear was equipped with anti-skid protection for slippery runway conditions. The 32-ply tires were coated with aluminum to reflect heat, and filled with high-pressure nitrogen. Depending upon the skill of the pilot, each tire was good for 15-20 landings. All Blackbirds used identical main landing gear, although this is an SR-71A (64-17973) at Blackbird Air Park. (Dennis R. Jenkins)

were almost as effective as elevons and rudders in influencing aircraft motion at high speeds. Inlet spike motion and bypass door operation could alter the aircraft's flight path under some conditions. The airflow dumped overboard through the inlet louvers entered a "stagnation area" just ahead of the louvers and actually flowed *forward* along the outside of the nacelle for a brief distance before mixing with the Mach 3 air stream and moving aft.

Most serious, however, was a problem that had earlier cropped up on

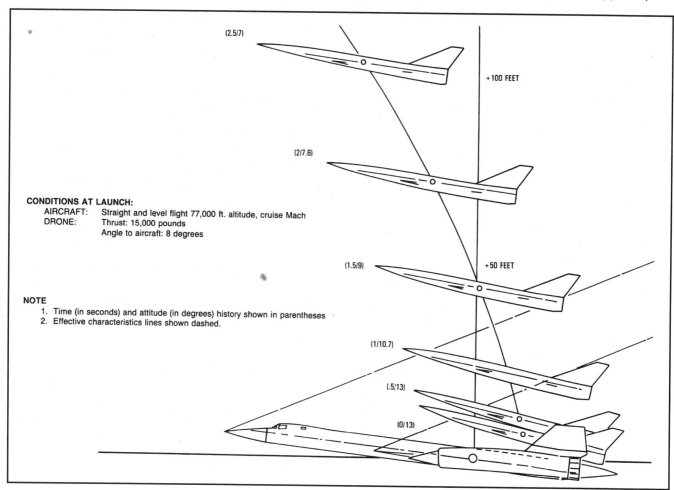

(2.5/7)

+100 FEET

(2/7.6)

CONDITIONS AT LAUNCH:
AIRCRAFT: Straight and level flight 77,000 ft. altitude, cruise Mach
DRONE: Thrust: 15,000 pounds
           Angle to aircraft: 8 degrees

(1.5/9)

+50 FEET

NOTE
1. Time (in seconds) and attitude (in degrees) history shown in parentheses
2. Effective characteristics lines shown dashed.

(1/10.7)

(.5/13)

(0/13)

Haven't we done this before? This model of a NASA SR-71 (YF-12C) shows an HT-4 hypersonic drone attached to the same location used by the D-21. NASA seriously considered launching this 50-foot long, 14,800 pound drone during 1971. Unlike the D-21, the HT-4 would have been stowed at a low angle-of-attack during acceleration. The nose of the drone would then be raised 8° and the entire drone moved aft almost a foot to guarantee at least 1g of upward acceleration upon launch. It was hoped that this would eliminate the problems encountered with the M-21 attempting to maintain a 0.9g downward arc during launch. (Tony Landis Collection)

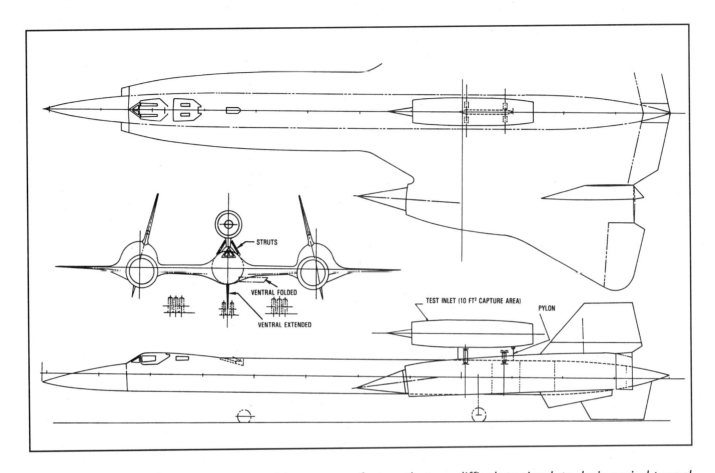

High performance inlet systems are sensitive to many factors that are difficult to simulate during wind tunnel testing of sub-scale models. NASA investigated using the YF-12A to carry a test version of a supersonic inlet. Various mounting techniques and location were considered, with this location being deemed most representative of the environment expected on a supersonic transport. Unfortunately, the SST program was cancelled and the test inlet was never built or flown, leaving many question unanswered. (NASA / DFRC)

the XB-70A – unwanted altitude changes, while cruising at high altitude and high speed. In fact, the main stability and control area of interest to NASA researchers was the ability to hold a desired cruise altitude. At high speeds and altitudes, without stability augmentation, the aircraft could change attitude slightly and since it was moving at Mach 3, any nose-up or nose-down change immediately produced major changes in altitude. The aircraft could enter porpoising motions for up to three minutes, during which altitudes could change by as much as ±3,000 feet. Such operation would certainly be prohibitive from an air traffic control standpoint with a commercial SST aircraft.

As one potential solution to the altitude-holding problem, FRC engineers developed a new autopilot for the YF-12A. Conventional autopilots adjust using thrust or moving aerodynamic control surfaces to maintain speed or altitude. The experimental YF-12 system linked the aircraft's central air-data computer to the autopilot, the inlet control system, and the engine throttle system. The combination of aerodynamic, inlet, and throttle control worked well on actual flight tests during extended high-Mach cruise. Such integrated systems would almost certainly be used on future SSTs.

By the early part of 1977, the NASA YF-12s had completed more than 175 flights with a good percentage at or above Mach 3. But the cost of flying the two high-performance aircraft became too great a burden for the FRC, and in the spring of 1977 NASA decided to retire the YF-12A and to return the YF-12C to the Air Force. The YF-12C was finally returned on 27 October 1978 and put into storage along with the nine remaining A-12s at Plant 42. The sole remaining YF-12A made its 146th and final flight to the Air Force Museum on 7 November 1979. With this the world's first and only Mach 3.0 fighter program came to an end.

DRONES OVER CHINA

TAGBOARD AND SENIOR BOWL

When originally conceived in early 1958, the A-12's primary mission was to overfly the Soviet Union. When Francis Gary Powers was shot down on 1 May 1960, the rules changed. One of the many concessions made by President Eisenhower for the release of Powers was the immediate cessation of all manned overflights. The word "manned" was carefully stipulated because of the possibilities envisioned for future reconnaissance satellites. However, since the satellites were still several years away from operations, the CIA determined that a drone also fell outside the "manned" category.

One of Skunk Works' first suggestions was to use a modified QF-104 launched from the back of an A-12. The CIA expressed absolutely no interest in this concept, so Lockheed went back to the drawing board. On 10 October 1962 the CIA authorized Lockheed to study a new drone code-named TAGBOARD specifically to overfly the Soviet Union and China. No detailed requirements appear to have been issued by the CIA, and Kelly Johnson was largely free to develop what he felt was necessary.

The vehicle had to be simple, relatively light-weight, capable of flight above Mach 3 at 90,000 feet, have a low radar cross-section, and be compatible with systems and techniques already developed for the A-12. One of the first decisions was to use a variation of the Blackbird's double-delta wing planform.

Because of the complexities of turbojet power and its associated intakes, the J58 was quickly discarded in favor of a Marquardt RJ43-MA-20-B4 ramjet. Since ramjet engines do not function at low speeds, a modified two-seat A-12 (designated M-21) was selected as a launch platform. The drone was originally known within Skunk Works as the Q-12. As work progressed however, it was given the

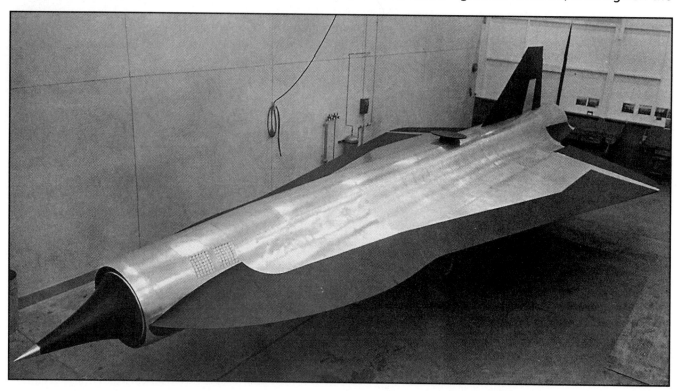

Lockheed built this mock-up of their Q-12 drone to gain Air Force approval for the program. The mock-up differed little from the production D-21 drones. Like the manned Blackbirds, the D-21 used titanium and composite construction. The CIA assigned the program the name of TAGBOARD. (Lockheed)

The D-21s used a Marquardt RJ43-MA-11 ramjet engine that provided 1,500 pounds-thrust and a speed of Mach 3.35 at 90,000 feet. This was the engine installation on the first D-21 (#501) during final assembly. A unique feature of ramjets is that they need to be moving comparatively fast before they will ignite, requiring release from a high-speed aircraft or rocket. Initially it was planned to use the M-21 for this purpose. (Lockheed)

D-21 designation, while its two-seat Blackbird launch vehicle was called the M-21. The "D" stood for "daughter" while the "M" meant "mother" – the "21" was simply "12" reversed to avoid confusion with other A-12 related projects. A full-scale mock-up of the drone was completed on 7 December 1962, and spent the next two weeks being tested for its radar cross-section.

The two M-21s were purpose-built, not modified A-12s, although there were remarkably few differences. A single dorsal-mounted pylon carried the D-21 but aerodynamic con-

(Above) A row of D-21 drones undergoing modification to D-21B standard at Lockheed. Only the first six drones were actually delivered as basic D-21s, and four of these were launched by the M-21s. The remaining drones were converted to the D-21B standard prior to their delivery to the Air Force for use by the modified SENIOR BOWL B-52Hs. (Lockheed)

Most of the plumbing and other components of the D-21B were accessible from the top. This D-21B is missing its flight control surfaces and all access panels while it sits in a work jig at Lockheed. The simple jig attached to the mounting locations on the bottom fuselage originally intended for the M-21 pylon, and the jig rotated to allow access to the top without the use of work stands. (Lockheed)

siderations resulted in the pylon being shorter than Kelly Johnson desired. This required that the M-21 "push over" during launch instead of flying straight and level as originally intended, a choice later regretted. The pylon contained a series of latches that secured the D-21 to the M-21, provisions for emergency pneumatic jettison of the D-21, and a refueling line that was used to top-off the drone's fuel tanks prior to launch. Unlike the original A-12s, the M-21 carried a back-seater known as the Launch Control Officer (LCO) who used a periscope to monitor the "daughter."

Only six inches of clearance existed between the D-21's wingtips and the top of the M-21's vertical stabilizers. The D-21 was placed to the rear of the normal center-of-gravity and a little nose high. Jettisonable nose and tail covers were installed to reduce the drag of the open, but non-functioning, inlet during early captive-carry flights. The inlet cover was angled down to assist the airflow over the M-21 and D-21.

The first "fit check" began on 19 June 1964 in Building 309/310 at Burbank using the first M-21 (60-6940) and the first D-21 (501). Very few problems were noted, and both the drone and mothership were cleared for final assembly. The first captive-carry flight occurred on 22 December 1964, ironically the same day that the first SR-71 made its maiden flight. The target date for the first launch was Kelly Johnson's birthday, 27 March 1965 but it did not quite work that way. Many problems needed to be worked through, and the first launch did not occur until 5 March 1966 over the Pacific Ocean somewhere between Pt. Mugu and Vandenberg AFB.

On the first launch attempt the drone's inlet cover was jettisoned and promptly collided with the leading edge of the D-21's wings, causing a great deal of damage. All future D-21 flights would be made without the covers, and the D-21's engine was usually started at Mach

The first D-21 drone (#501) was moved under the cover of darkness from its manufacturing area in Burbank building 82 to the Blackbird assembly area in building 309/310 for the first mating of the drone to its M-21 (60-6940) mothership. Surprisingly, the fit-check disclosed no unexpected problems. At this point the drone was missing its outer wing panels and vertical stabilizer. Noteworthy are the M-21's outer wing panels which are partially open to allow access to the engine compartments. (Lockheed)

Originally the plan was for the D-21 to have aerodynamic inlet and exhaust covers to assist the M-21 in reaching its desired launch speed. These covers would be pyrotechnically jettisoned immediately prior to launch. This photograph shows the result of the first, and last, attempt to jettison the nose fairing. Debris from the fairing impacted the composite leading edge of the drone, severely damaging it. All future flights would delete the cover, and use the drone's engine to provide the M-21 with some additional thrust to compensate for the extra drag. The drone's fuel tanks would be topped-off in flight from the M-21. (Lockheed)

The first test flight of the D-21 (#501) mated to the M-21 (60-6940) occurred on 22 December 1964. The drone's intake cover is clearly visible. Lockheed test pilot Bill Park was flying the M-21, and the back seat was empty as a safety precaution. An F-104, in this case flown by Art Peterson, was used for chase on most Lockheed test flights. (Lockheed)

Like all the other Blackbirds, the M-21 was capable of in-flight refueling, and in fact, its mission profile dictated at least two refuelings. The 11,000 pound drone on its back, and the aerodynamic interaction of the drone and the tanker's boom, made it a chore for the M-21 pilot to take on fuel even in calm skies. (Lockheed)

1.24 to eliminate some induced drag, and also to provide additional power to achieve the desired launch speed.

The mated combination was not as straight-forward as it might appear. The added weight of the D-21 significantly slowed the acceleration of the Blackbird. To be at the correct speed and altitude over Pt. Mugu, the M-21 had to begin its speed run over Albuquerque, New Mexico. Once the Marquardt ramjet was running at full power, the M-21 was flown downward in a 0.9g arc to assist in separation. Fuel reserves were minimal when the M-21 reached the launch point, and an in-flight refueling had to be made immediately after the drone was launched (or immediately after the decision was made not to launch it).

The M-21's spent their entire career in natural metal finish with the normal black composite areas. This is the first flight on 22 December 1964. Even though they were CIA aircraft, all the A-12 series aircraft carried full U.S. Air Force markings. (Lockheed)

The first successful launch from an M-21 was made on 5 March 1966 with the drone having only 25% of its design fuel load. A launch with a 50% fuel load was made on 27 April 1966, while a full fuel launch was

The first test fitting of a D-21B (#507) to a SENIOR BOWL pylon was accomplished on 1 June 1967 in Burbank building 82. The drone is still missing its engine and wing leading edges, and many access panels are missing from the pylon. The structure in the nose intake is noteworthy. (Lockheed)

One of the SENIOR BOWL B-52Hs (61-0021) carrying two D-21B drones, one under each wing. The B-52s carried Vietnam-era camouflage throughout the program. A camera port was installed on each side of the B-52's forward fuselage, and a camera was also located in each launch pylon. (Lockheed)

made on 16 June 1966. The full fuel load enabled the drone to fly almost 1,600 miles while making eight programmed turns and maneuvers.

Lockheed test pilot Bill Park did not believe that a sustained 0.9g arc could be maintained under the pressure of an operational mission. In an attempt to determine how critical it was to maintain exactly 0.9g, a scheduled 30 July 1966 full fuel launch would attempt separation while pulling 1.0g – a crucial mistake. As the D-21 passed through the M-21's bow wake, it experienced an "asymmetrical unstart" situation where the ramjet's flame holder lost the right side of the fuel burn, causing the D-21 (#504) to roll to the right at separation. As a result, the M-21 pitched up uncontrollably. Bill Park pushed the control stick full nose down in an attempt to correct the situation, but the D-21 impacted the M-21 at Mach 3.25, destroying the mothership's right rudder, right engine nacelle, and most of the outer wing panel. The Blackbird tumbled out of

A D-21B shortly after release from a SENIOR BOWL B-52H. This photograph was taken from the pylon camera. The solid-fuel rocket motor has not yet ignited. One of the few visual clues between the original D-21 and the D-21B was the large air data tube on each wing leading edge. (Lockheed)

One of the surviving D-21Bs has been placed on display at the Blackbird Air Park in Palmdale, California, mounted on its special trailer assembly. The blended aft fuselage assisted in managing flow separation around the exhaust nozzle, and also helped the drone's "stealth" characteristics. (Dennis R. Jenkins)

The nozzle on the D-21B was less complex than the manned Blackbirds since it did not have to deal with the sensitivities of a turbojet engine or a varied flight regime (the D-21s only operated at supersonic speeds). The D-21B added a large air data probe on each wing leading edge, in addition to the one in the center of the inlet spike. Bleed air was exhausted by two small vents on each side of the intake. (Dennis R. Jenkins)

control and into the Pacific. Both Park and Ray Torick successfully ejected, but Torick's pressure suit was torn during the ejection, filling with water immediately upon landing. Torick drowned before rescue teams could arrive on the scene.

The M-21-launch portion of TAG-BOARD was terminated in August 1966. Kelly Johnson had been sure the drone would make a valuable reconnaissance asset and had already initiated preliminary studies of using a rocket to accelerate the D-21 to speed after launch from a larger aircraft. The remaining D-21

The D-21B (#525) on display at the Palmdale Air Park is actually owned by NASA/Dryden but will probably never be used for future flight research. The Air Park also has an A-12, SR-71, and J58 engine on display. (Dennis R. Jenkins)

The first knowledge the general public had that the D-21 even existed was when a wind storm blew canvas tarps off of some drones stored at Davis-Monthan AFB on the same day that an aviation

photography group was on the base. Exactly what the drones were was open for speculation for a time, although it was obvious they were in some way related to the Lockheed Blackbirds. The white covering is "spraylat," a protective latex covering that is used to seal any openings in aircraft stored in the desert. (Dennis R. Jenkins)

WARBIRD**TECH**
S E R I E S

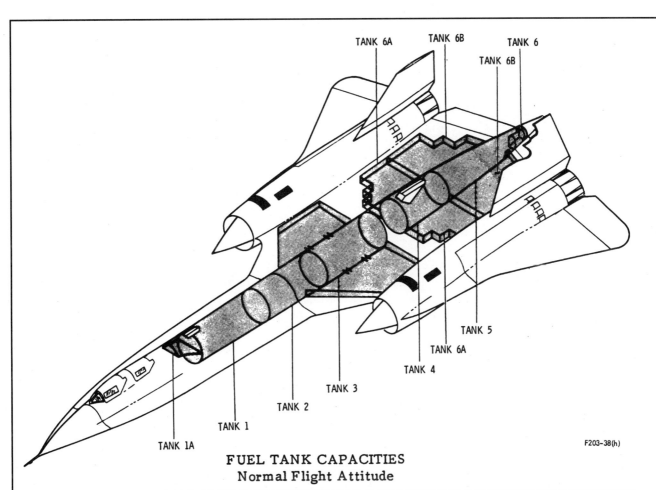

TANK 6A   TANK 6B   TANK 6

TANK 6B

TANK 5

TANK 6A

TANK 4

TANK 3

TANK 2

TANK 1

TANK 1A

F203-38(h)

FUEL TANK CAPACITIES
Normal Flight Attitude

Tank	Fuel/Gal	Fuel (JP-7)
1A	251.1	1650 lb.
1	2095.9	13770 lb.
2	1974.1	12970 lb.
3	2459.7	16160 lb.
4	1453.6	9550 lb.
5	1758.0	11550 lb.
6A (forward)	1158.3	7610 lb.
6B (Aft)	1068.5	7020 lb.
Total	12219.2	80280 lb. *

* At average fuel density of 6.57 lb./gal.
(46.2° API, Fuel temperature = 78°F)

The SR-71 was capable of carrying 12,219.2 gallons of JP-7 in six major fuselage tanks. At an average weight of 6.57 pounds per gallon this translated to 80, 280 pounds of fuel. The Blackbirds seldom took-off with a full fuel load due to fuel leakage, tire and brake heating, abort criteria, and single engine performance restrictions. The usual load was between 45,000-65,000 pounds and most Blackbird missions involved several aerial refuelings. (U.S. Air Force)

This was the D-21 configuration during early flight tests. The original D-21 did not have the large air data probes on the wing leading edges seen on later D-21Bs. The protective inlet cover was only used on early captive-carry flights since it proved destructive to the drone's leading edges when it was jettisoned. The camera compartment hatch outline can barely be discerned under the drone, as can the single faired-over camera port (on the v-shaped portion of the hatch).
(Tony Landis Collection)

drones were modified under project SENIOR BOWL for launch from Boeing B-52Hs and redesignated D-21B. Two B-52Hs were modified to carry the D-21B, and would conduct a total of 17 launches and four operational missions prior to the program being terminated on 23 July 1971.

The existence of the D-21 was also the Blackbird's best kept secret. It existed for over ten years, in fact it had been removed from service, before the public accidentally discovered it. Seventeen D-21s had been retired to Davis-Monthan AFB near Tucson, Arizona, and dutifully covered by tarps to protect them

from prying eyes. A chance windstorm blew some of the covers off the drones on the same morning that a group of aviation enthusiasts were taking a tour of the storage area. Photographs of the D-21s appeared in *Aviation Week* shortly thereafter.

Two D-21Bs and their boosters weighed a total of 48,572 pounds – a heavy load even for a B-52H. Here the first D-21 (#501) is shown under the wing of one of the SENIOR BOWL B-52Hs. This drone was later lost when it was accidentally dropped from the wing of its B-52H. (Lockheed)

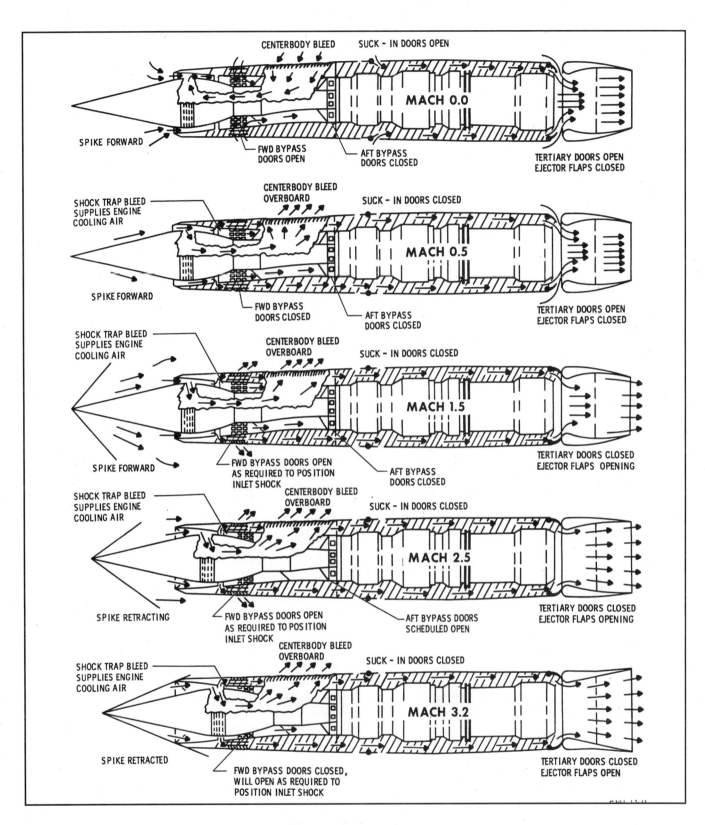

CENTERBODY BLEED   SUCK - IN DOORS OPEN

MACH 0.0

SPIKE FORWARD

FWD BYPASS DOORS OPEN   AFT BYPASS DOORS CLOSED

TERTIARY DOORS OPEN EJECTOR FLAPS CLOSED

SHOCK TRAP BLEED SUPPLIES ENGINE COOLING AIR

CENTERBODY BLEED OVERBOARD   SUCK - IN DOORS CLOSED

MACH 0.5

SPIKE FORWARD

FWD BYPASS DOORS CLOSED   AFT BYPASS DOORS CLOSED

TERTIARY DOORS OPEN EJECTOR FLAPS CLOSED

SHOCK TRAP BLEED SUPPLIES ENGINE COOLING AIR

CENTERBODY BLEED OVERBOARD   SUCK - IN DOORS CLOSED

MACH 1.5

SPIKE FORWARD

FWD BYPASS DOORS OPEN AS REQUIRED TO POSITION INLET SHOCK   AFT BYPASS DOORS CLOSED

TERTIARY DOORS CLOSED EJECTOR FLAPS OPENING

SHOCK TRAP BLEED SUPPLIES ENGINE COOLING AIR

CENTERBODY BLEED OVERBOARD   SUCK - IN DOORS CLOSED

MACH 2.5

SPIKE RETRACTING

FWD BYPASS DOORS OPEN AS REQUIRED TO POSITION INLET SHOCK   AFT BYPASS DOORS SCHEDULED OPEN

TERTIARY DOORS CLOSED EJECTOR FLAPS OPENING

SHOCK TRAP BLEED SUPPLIES ENGINE COOLING AIR

CENTERBODY BLEED OVERBOARD   SUCK - IN DOORS CLOSED

MACH 3.2

SPIKE RETRACTED

FWD BYPASS DOORS CLOSED, WILL OPEN AS REQUIRED TO POSITION INLET SHOCK

TERTIARY DOORS CLOSED EJECTOR FLAPS OPEN

The Blackbird inlets provided over 80 percent of the total thrust at Mach 3.2 cruise. Each inlet had a large spike that was used to control and position the supersonic air flow at the throat of the inlet for optimum performance and to prevent supersonic air from entering the engine. A series of doors and vents along the inlet were used to relieve excess air pressure from inside the inlet. The forward bypass doors created a tremendous amount of drag on the aircraft as the slower air exiting hit the supersonic air stream. For this reason the forward doors were kept closed as much as possible. (U.S. Air Force)

THE SENIOR CROWN

AN OXCART IN A BLUE SUIT

In December 1962 the Air Force ordered six "reconnaissance-strike" versions of the Blackbird optimized to conduct high-speed, high altitude reconnaissance of enemy territory after a nuclear strike. In August 1963, the Air Force added 25 more aircraft to the SENIOR CROWN contract, for a total of 31.

Internally Lockheed referred to the new aircraft as the R-12, a reconfigured A-12 that was slightly longer and heavier to accommodate different reconnaissance systems and a second crew member. The "Q" bay which housed the A-12's very capable camera system became the cockpit for the reconnaissance systems officer (RSO). The Air Force wanted an aircraft capable of using side-looking radar in addition to using several different cameras and incorporating the ability to collect Signal Intelligence (SIGINT). The additional weight of all this equipment resulted in a slower maximum speed and a lower operating ceiling.

The 31 SR-71s were manufactured in the same area previously used for the OXCART aircraft and YF-12As. This photograph shows two aft fuselage and wing structures being built-up side-by-side. The one on the left is further along, with most of the fuselage skin being in place. The one in the lower right corner shows technicians installing fuselage bulkheads, although most of the engine nacelle is already skinned. (Lockheed)

The forward fuselages were built-up separately from the rest of the airframe. Noteworthy are the protective panels placed over the chines to protect the composite skin during assembly. The open compartment immediately aft of the second cockpit is for the star tracker and will eventually contain a nine-inch diameter quartz window. (Lockheed)

Three SR-71s in building 309/310 in Burbank. This was not so much an assembly line as a space on the factory floor where final assembly took place. The aircraft did not move once in this location until they were completed. The center aircraft already has its vertical stabilizers installed, although the other two aircraft do not. The upper wing skin was closed up last, allowing access to wires, cables, and fluid lines until the last minute. (Lockheed)

The first mockup review of the R-12 was on 13/14 June 1963 with a final review on 11 December 1963. By mid-March 1964 the construction of the first six R-12s was well underway and around the same time the Air Force designated the aircraft RS-71, following the still-born RS-70 version of the XB-70 strategic bomber.

The process of making public the various versions of the Blackbird continued on 25 July 1964, when President Johnson revealed the existence of a new Air Force reconnaissance aircraft, which he called the "SR-71" instead of "RS-71." Deciding that renaming the aircraft was easier than correcting the President, the Air Force invented a new category ("strategic reconnaissance") to explain the SR-71's designation.

At the end of October 1964 the first SR-71A (64-17950) was ready to begin the overland journey followed by all Blackbirds. But unlike

The SR-71s were transported out of Burbank using the same specially-built trailers as the OXCARTs and YF-12As. The major difference was that the SR-71s were taken to Palmdale for their first flights instead of Groom Lake. (Lockheed)

An outer wing being attached. Each nacelle was split down its centerline, with the outer half of the nacelle and entire outer wing panel swinging up to provide access to the engine. A J58 waits in the foreground. The small holes on the trailing edge of the outer wing panel are attachment locations for the elevon and its actuators. (Lockheed)

An SR-71 undergoing heavy maintenance. Most of the upper wing skin and the upper chine skin has been removed. It is easy to distinguish this from a photograph from the original production line since the aircraft is painted black. There was remarkably little structure under the chines. (Lockheed)

the A-12 and YF-12s before it, the journey would lead to new Lockheed facilities located at Air Force Plant 42 in Palmdale, California, only 50 miles from Burbank. All the earlier aircraft had gone to Groom Lake for their first flights. The SR-71 would use Plant 42, which is officially known as the Production Flight Test Facility. In the early morning darkness of 29 October 1964 the SR-71 departed Burbank aboard one of the same specially-

Most maintenance was accomplished in the special hangers at Beale AFB where the SR-71s lived. This aircraft is missing most of the bottom skin on the nose unit. There were several different nose section available, depending on the reconnaissance equipment required for a particular mission. (Lockheed)

One of the upper wing "blend" panels has been removed from this SR-71, showing the contours of the fuel tank that makes up most of the fuselage structure. This area is primarily shaped the way it is for aerodynamic and radar-defeating reasons, and very little use of the volume was made since the temperatures were high and insulation would have added considerable weight. (Lockheed)

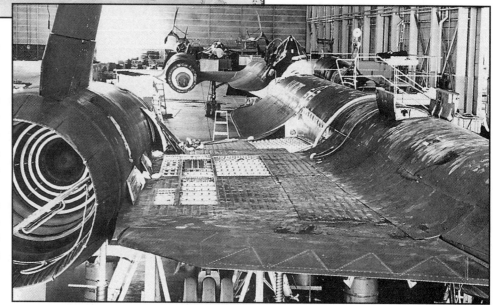

WARBIRD**TECH**
S E R I E S

The first SR-71A (64-17950) is readied for its first flight from Palmdale. The small white marking on the nose was a distinguishing feature of this aircraft during its early flight test career. (Lockheed)

developed trailers used by all other Blackbirds.

The aircraft's first flight took place on 22 December 1964 with Lockheed test pilot Robert J. Gilliland at the controls and an empty back seat. The flight lasted just over an hour, and attained a maximum speed of slightly over 1,000 MPH – not bad for a first flight! On the same day, 150 miles to the north east, the M-21 mothership was making its first flight from Groom Lake.

Just over a year later, on 7 January

The first SR-71B (64-17956) trainer celebrated its 1,000th mission on 15 January 1982. To commemorate the occasion the Air Force painted special 1,000th mission markings on the belly and vertical stabilizers (although they could not agree whether it was a "mission," "sortie," or "flight"). (Lockheed)

The SR-71 trainers (two SR-71Bs and a single SR-71C) featured a raised aft cockpit for the instructor pilot. Although visually similar to the forward one, the aft canopy does not have a separate windscreen, the entire unit being hinged. Visibility was not great and it was fortunate that all SR-71 "students" were otherwise experienced pilots. The aft canopy on the SR-71 trainers was decidedly different than the aft cockpit in the "Titanium Goose" OXCART trainer. (Lockheed)

The first SR-71A (64-17950) was retained by Lockheed as a test aircraft for its entire career. This aircraft was written off in an accident at Edwards AFB on 10 January 1967 when several tires failed during an antiskid braking test. The tires caught fire which quickly spread to the rest of the aircraft. Lockheed test pilot Art Peterson survived. Two other SR-71As (64-17954 and 17977) would be lost within two years due to landing gear failures, leading Lockheed and the Air Force to develop more robust wheels and tires. (Lockheed)

Another SR-71A (64-17955) was retained at Palmdale as an engineering test aircraft. This aircraft wore a white "Skunk Works" logo on its tail for its entire career. The aircraft is currently reserved for eventual display at Edwards AFB. (Lockheed)

1966 the Air Force took delivery of its first SR-71, a modified SR-71B trainer (64-19756) at Beale AFB, California. The first mission-capable SR-71 was the tenth aircraft manufactured (64-17958), delivered to Beale AFB on 4 April 1966. All thirty-one of the original SR-71s would be delivered by the end of 1967. A thirty-second aircraft, the sole SR-71C (64-17981), would be assembled later after the second SR-71B trainer was lost in an accident on 11 January 1968. The SR-71C would be constructed using the aft fuselage and wings from the first YF-12A which had been written-off in a landing accident at Edwards, and the forward fuselage from the SR-71 structural test article (hence its Lockheed number

America's premier reconnaissance platforms both originated within Lockheed Skunk Works. The SR-71A is in the foreground, while a U-2R (probably called a TR-1 when this photo was taken) is in the background. The two represented very different approaches to the same basic problem. It is somewhat ironic that the Blackbird was developed as a successor to the U-2, then retired before the U-2. (Lockheed)

The SR-71 had nine compartments that usually carried mission equipment. The nose compartment was the largest of these and could house either optical cameras or radar equipment. Four mission bays were located in the chine area on either side of the fuselage behind the second cockpit. While the SR-71A was operational it almost always carried very high-resolution Technical Objective Cameras (TEOC) in the forward left and right mission bays. The cameras could be pointed from zero to 45 degrees to the side of the aircraft. At a zero pointing angle the TEOCs covered a 2.4 NM square area. The aircraft carried sufficient film to photograph 1,428 NM. Some of the more interesting photographs taken by the TEOCs were of various MiGs falling back to Earth after failed intercepts. (U.S. Air Force)

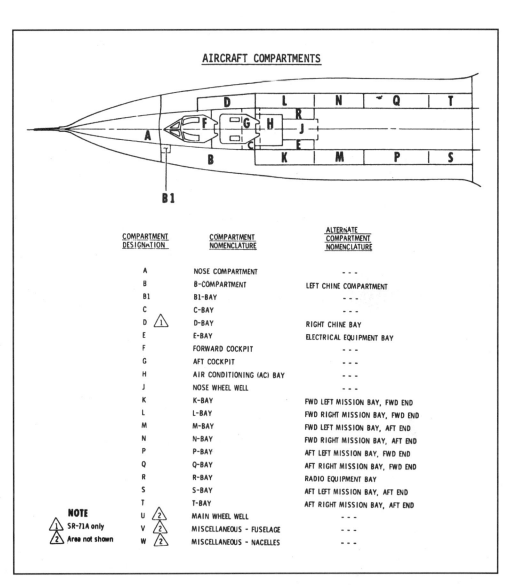

AIRCRAFT COMPARTMENTS

COMPARTMENT DESIGNATION	COMPARTMENT NOMENCLATURE	ALTERNATE COMPARTMENT NOMENCLATURE
A	NOSE COMPARTMENT	- - -
B	B-COMPARTMENT	LEFT CHINE COMPARTMENT
B1	B1-BAY	- - -
C	C-BAY	- - -
D △1	D-BAY	RIGHT CHINE BAY
E	E-BAY	ELECTRICAL EQUIPMENT BAY
F	FORWARD COCKPIT	- - -
G	AFT COCKPIT	- - -
H	AIR CONDITIONING (AC) BAY	- - -
J	NOSE WHEEL WELL	- - -
K	K-BAY	FWD LEFT MISSION BAY, FWD END
L	L-BAY	FWD RIGHT MISSION BAY, FWD END
M	M-BAY	FWD LEFT MISSION BAY, AFT END
N	N-BAY	FWD RIGHT MISSION BAY, AFT END
P	P-BAY	AFT LEFT MISSION BAY, FWD END
Q	Q-BAY	AFT RIGHT MISSION BAY, FWD END
R	R-BAY	RADIO EQUIPMENT BAY
S	S-BAY	AFT LEFT MISSION BAY, AFT END
T	T-BAY	AFT RIGHT MISSION BAY, AFT END
U △2	MAIN WHEEL WELL	- - -
V △2	MISCELLANEOUS - FUSELAGE	- - -
W △2	MISCELLANEOUS - NACELLES	- - -

NOTE
△1 SR-71A only
△2 Area not shown

The protruding aft fuselage of the SR-71 shows up here. This was one of the most noticeable differences between the SR-71 and earlier Blackbirds although the chine shape was also different. Surprisingly, several SR-71As sported tail art during their careers, including 64-17976 with a stylized cat motif. (Lockheed)

Towards the end of its operational career the SR-71 gave up on the white "U.S. Air Force" and serial number markings. Here the markings consist entirely of a subdued red serial number on the tail. (Lockheed)

#2000). The SR-71C was not well thought of, and spent most of its career in flyable storage, used only when the surviving SR-71B was down for maintenance. The C-model did have a desirable attribute, however, since it was somewhat lighter than other SR-71s and accelerated faster. It also was not, apparently, constructed quite 'square,' and was in a constant yaw at supersonic speeds.

Of the 32 SR-71s built, the first six were used for flight tests (three dedicated to Lockheed and three to the Air Force), while the 7th, 8th and 32nd aircraft were trainers and not capable of operational reconnaissance missions. That left 25 operational SR-71As, 20 percent of which were out of service at any given time undergoing major overhauls or modifications at Palmdale, or down for maintenance at their operating location.

The nose chines of the SR-71 were fuller and rounder than those of the OXCART aircraft. This provided some additional lift to help compensate for the increased weight the SR-71 carried around and also provided additional internal volume for new mission equipment. The aft fuselage extension cured some parasitic drag found to exist on the earlier aircraft. (Lockheed)

WARBIRD**TECH**
S E R I E S

Therefore sixteen SR-71As could be operational at any given time, which worked out to two squadrons of nine aircraft (eight SR-71As, plus a trainer each). These two squadrons, the 1st Strategic Reconnaissance Squadron (SRS) and the 99th SRS were organized under the 9th Strategic Reconnaissance Wing (SRW) at Beale AFB. Four other locations would also play host to the Blackbirds as needed: Edwards AFB, California, for testing by the 4786th Test Squadron; Det 1 of the 9th SRW at Kadena AB, Okinawa, using facilities originally constructed for the CIA's A-12; Det 4 of the 9th SRW at Mildenhall Royal Air Force Base, England; and Det 51 of the 9th SRW at Plant 42. Det 51 was responsible for flight testing the aircraft as they were manufactured, and after significant overhauls and modifications performed by Lockheed at Palmdale. Det 51 was actually a sub-unit of Det 6 at Norton AFB which reported to the 2762nd Logistics

All of the Blackbirds were capable of aerial refueling. Here an SR-71A (64-17968) takes on fuel from a KC-135. For years the Blackbirds had a dedicated fleet of KC-135Q tankers to meet their needs for JP-7 and were equipped with special radios for communicating with the Blackbirds. Towards the end of their careers, the Blackbirds were refueled from regular KC-135A/E/R tankers, as well as KC-10As, at least while they were operating in the United States. (Lockheed)

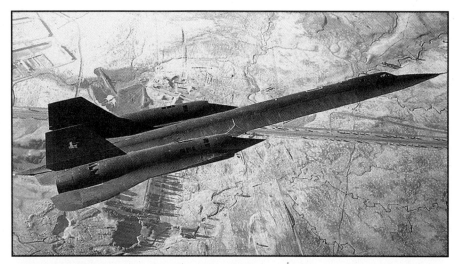

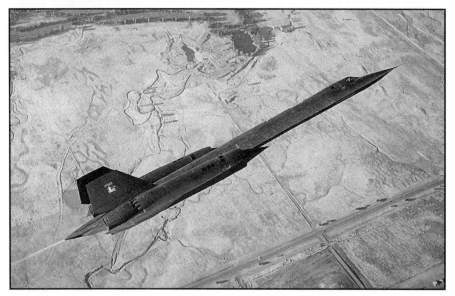

Like most aircraft the SR-71's dumped fuel at the last moment to get within approved landing weights. Here 64-17968 banks as it returns to Beale AFB in northern California. By this time the SR-71s were using subdued red markings in place of their earlier white ones. (Lockheed)

Tail art also adorned 64-17968. For most of their careers the only "sanctioned" tail art was the "Skunk Works" logos carried on the aircraft used by Lockheed. While the aircraft were operating from overseas bases the crews frequently painted a small piece of art on the tail, but these were generally removed prior to returning Stateside. (Lockheed)

Squadron, and was responsible for the SR-71's logistics system.

Without aerial refueling, the range of the SR-71 was limited to approximately 2,000 miles at operational speeds. Multiple aerial refuelings could extended the range of the aircraft past the practical limit of the crew's endurance, and missions of 12,000 miles were not uncommon. A total of 35 Boeing Stratotankers were modified to the KC-135Q configuration used by the Blackbirds. All the aircraft were assigned to the 349th and 350th Aerial Refueling Squadrons at Beale.

The Q-model tankers differed from regular KC-135s in having some special plumbing to allow the carriage of both JP-4 and JP-7, modified engines that could burn either fuel, and the capability to supply (via hoses) fuel to the SR-71s while on the ground (in case a Blackbird landed somewhere without JP-7 available). In addition, special (text continued on page 69)

The heat from the J58 engines completely distorts the background as this SR-71A taxies towards its hanger at Beale AFB. The unique three-wheeled main landing gear effectively carried the weight of this 100,000+ pound aircraft. The inward cant of the vertical stabilizers was an effort to defeat radar detection. (Lockheed)

THE COLOR OF BLACK

The ability of the Blackbird to achieve high-altitude high-Mach flight derives from its propulsion system and its structure, which is 93% titanium alloy with the remainder consisting of high-temperature composite materials. The black paint, in addition to reportedly absorbing some radar signals, assists in the reduction of internal temperatures during high-speed flight. Virtually every part and component of the aircraft and its systems were specifically designed and fabricated to withstand the rigorous conditions dictated by its flight envelope.

The third YF-12A (60-6936) and a GAR-9 (AIM-47) missile. This was after May 1965, evidenced by the three record marks (white Blackbird silhouettes) on the nose. The IRST sensors have been removed from the chines. (Lockheed)

The SR-71 production line in Burbank during mid-1965. Five Blackbirds can be seen in various stages of completion. The closest aircraft appears to have metal rudders, while the third aircraft in might have composite units fitted. For unexplained reasons the Air Force was reluctant to use the composite rudders on the SR-71, although the CIA did not experience any unexpected problems with them on the A-12. (Lockheed)

This was the first photo of an A-12 cleared by the CIA for release in 1982. Somewhat unusually this shows an all-black A-12 (60-6932) with unpainted metal vertical stabilizers. This particular aircraft was lost on 5 June 1968 near the Philippine Islands. The pilot, Jack Weeks, was never found and presumed killed in the accident. (Lockheed)

A line-up of Blackbirds on the ramp at Groom lake. The closest aircraft is the first A-12 (69-6924), followed by the "Titanium Goose" two-seater then six more single-seat A-12s. The last two aircraft are the first two YF-12A interceptors. At this point all the Blackbirds were still mostly unpainted. A mixture of metal and composite vertical stabilizers can be seen. Other versions of this photo had the mountains in the background airbrushed out in an attempt to disguise the test location. (Lockheed)

Externally the M-21 (60-6940) was virtually identical to the single-seat A-12 except for the small window in the second canopy and the launch pylon for the D-21. This is another photograph from the first captive carry flight showing the streamline nose and tail cones on the drone. (Lockheed)

One of NASA's SR-71As (64-17980) shows the unique afterburner shock waves generated by the Blackbirds. As of 1997 there are four Blackbirds flying out of Edwards AFB, two operated by the Air Force and two operated by NASA. It is still an awe inspiring sight to watch the SR-71s take-off over the desert in the early morning or late evening. (NASA / DFRC)

After being turned over to NASA the second YF-12A (60-6935) spent some time without NASA markings. The interceptor version was the only Blackbird to feature a raised cockpit area for the pilot, a somewhat unsuccessful attempt to provide better visibility. (Tony Landis Collection)

An A-12 (60-6933) sits parked in front of the OXCART hangers at Groom Lake. The distinctive natural metal and black paint scheme was initially applied to all the OXCART aircraft and the YF-12As. The black covers the high-temperature plastic composite areas of the wing leading edges and fuselage chines, as well as the composite vertical stabilizers. Black paint was extended around the cockpit partially to provide better heat radiance, and partially simply as an anti-glare shield. (Lockheed via Tony Landis)

The YF-12A's back cockpit contained the radar controls (lower right) and missile controls (lower left), as well as the large radar scope and map displays. The back seater could not fly the aircraft; in fact, he could barely see out of the aircraft! (Lockheed)

Unlike most aircraft, the Blackbird cruised in afterburner, although this photograph was taken as the aircraft accelerated after a tanking. The shiny streaks under the wings are JP-7 leaks. (NASA via Tony Landis)

The first M-21 (60-6940) on the ramp at Groom Lake. This aircraft never actually launched a D-21 although it was used for the initial captive-carry flights and as the photo chase aircraft for the four launches from the other M-21 (60-6941). This aircraft is now on display at The Museum of Flight in Seattle. (Lockheed)

Three distinctly different nose sections were available for the SR-71A. One of these was essentially an empty shell for use when no mission equipment was required. The other two were an Optical Bar Camera (OBC) nose that contained a high-resolution panoramic camera, and a radar nose section with a side-looking radar system known as CAPRE (Capability Reconnaissance). The OBC's terrain coverage was 2 NM along the ground track and extended 36 NM to each side of the aircraft. Sufficient film was carried to cover approximately 2,952 NM, or half that in the stereo mode. In 1986 an additional nose was introduced, this one carrying an Advanced Synthetic Aperture Radar System (ASARS). In the search mode the ASARS could "see" a 10 NM wide swath positioned 20-100 NM to the left or right of the ground track. The ASARS nose could be identified by two small "dimples" in the chines. (U.S. Air Force)

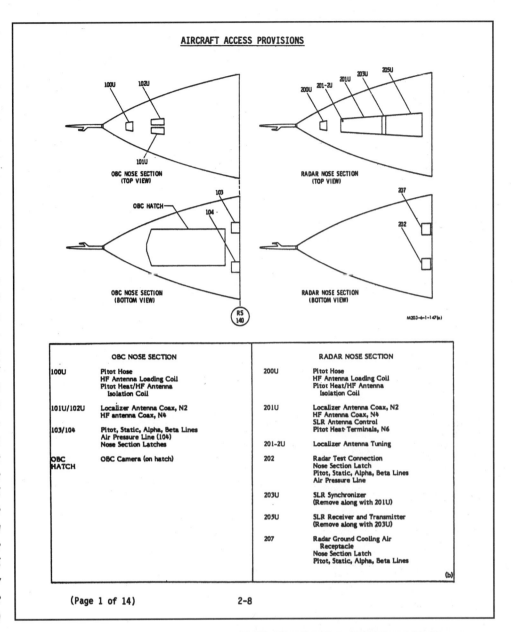

AIRCRAFT ACCESS PROVISIONS

OBC NOSE SECTION (TOP VIEW)

RADAR NOSE SECTION (TOP VIEW)

OBC NOSE SECTION (BOTTOM VIEW)

RADAR NOSE SECTION (BOTTOM VIEW)

OBC NOSE SECTION		RADAR NOSE SECTION	
100U	Pitot Hose HF Antenna Loading Coil Pitot Heat/HF Antenna Isolation Coil	200U	Pitot Hose HF Antenna Loading Coil Pitot Heat/HF Antenna Isolation Coil
101U/102U	Localizer Antenna Coax, N2 HF antenna Coax, N4	201U	Localizer Antenna Coax, N2 HF Antenna Coax, N4 SLR Antenna Control Pitot Heat Terminals, N6
103/104	Pitot, Static, Alpha, Beta Lines Air Pressure Line (104) Nose Section Latches	201-2U	Localizer Antenna Tuning
OBC HATCH	OBC Camera (on hatch)	202	Radar Test Connection Nose Section Latch Pitot, Static, Alpha, Beta Lines Air Pressure Line
		203U	SLR Synchronizer (Remove along with 201U)
		205U	SLR Receiver and Transmitter (Remove along with 203U)
		207	Radar Ground Cooling Air Receptacle Nose Section Latch Pitot, Static, Alpha, Beta Lines

(Page 1 of 14)   2-8

(text continued from page 64) AN/ARC-50 radios were installed that allowed variable power transmissions as well as secure (encrypted) communications.

Early in the program it was not uncommon for the Air Force to dis-

All SR-71s carried a UHF antenna on the lower fuselage while operating in the United States. This antenna was often outlined with a white semi-circle and was located on the right side of the aircraft immediately ahead of the nose gear well. (Troy Downen)

After several years of service a "heat dispersion" plate was added to the forward windscreen. Visibility from the forward cockpit was not terrific, especially when the thickness of the glass was considered. Only the left side was equipped with a defroster/anti-ice equipment. However, there was not all that much to look at at 80,000 feet anyway. (Lockheed)

patch as many as three tankers to support a single Blackbird refueling, providing sufficient fuel plus a spare tanker in case of problems aboard one of the others. Late in the program budgetary considerations reduced this type of support, and it was not uncommon for only a single tanker to be available. The tankers could refuel a Blackbird at approximately 6,000 pounds of JP-7 per minute at a pressure of 65-70 PSI and a complete refueling took approximately 15 minutes. Very late in the program the Blackbirds lost their dedicated tanker support and used whatever tanker came up in rotation, including standard KC-135A/E/R and KC-10As.

An SR-71A poses with some of the reconnaissance equipment that it can carry. Unlike the OXCART which carried only photographic equipment, the SR-71 could carry a full range of photographic, radar, and signal intelligence collecting equipment. This was ultimately why the SR-71 was selected instead of the A-12 to remain in service, since it provided a wider variety of intelligence capabilities. It should be noted, however, that its photographic capabilities were somewhat limited compared to OXCART which could carry larger (and hence better) cameras in the "Q" bay that houses the SR-71s second seat. (Lockheed via Tony Landis)

WARBIRD**TECH**
SERIES

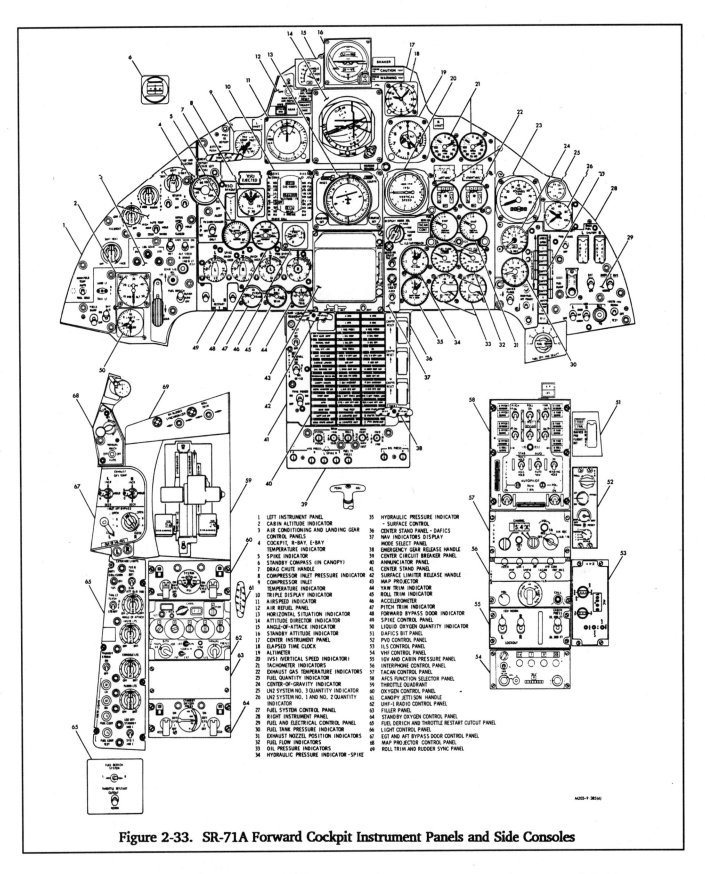

Figure 2-33. SR-71A Forward Cockpit Instrument Panels and Side Consoles

1   LEFT INSTRUMENT PANEL
2   CABIN ALTITUDE INDICATOR
3   AIR CONDITIONING AND LANDING GEAR
    CONTROL PANELS
4   COCKPIT, R-BAY, E-BAY
    TEMPERATURE INDICATOR
5   SPIKE INDICATOR
6   STANDBY COMPASS (IN CANOPY)
7   DRAG CHUTE HANDLE
8   COMPRESSOR INLET PRESSURE INDICATOR
9   COMPRESSOR INLET
    TEMPERATURE INDICATOR
10 TRIPLE DISPLAY INDICATOR
11 AIRSPEED INDICATOR
12 AIR REFUEL PANEL
13 HORIZONTAL SITUATION INDICATOR
14 ATTITUDE DIRECTOR INDICATOR
15 ANGLE-OF-ATTACK INDICATOR
16 STANDBY ATTITUDE INDICATOR
17 CENTER INSTRUMENT PANEL
18 ELAPSED TIME CLOCK
19 ALTIMETER
20 IVSI (VERTICAL SPEED INDICATOR)
21 TACHOMETER INDICATORS
22 EXHAUST GAS TEMPERATURE INDICATORS
23 FUEL QUANTITY INDICATOR
24 CENTER-OF-GRAVITY INDICATOR
25 LN2 SYSTEM NO. 3 QUANTITY INDICATOR
26 LN2 SYSTEM NO. 1 AND NO. 2 QUANTITY
    INDICATOR
27 FUEL SYSTEM CONTROL PANEL
28 RIGHT INSTRUMENT PANEL
29 FUEL AND ELECTRICAL CONTROL PANEL
30 FUEL TANK PRESSURE INDICATOR
31 EXHAUST NOZZLE POSITION INDICATORS
32 FUEL FLOW INDICATORS
33 OIL PRESSURE INDICATORS
34 HYDRAULIC PRESSURE INDICATOR - SPIKE

35 HYDRAULIC PRESSURE INDICATOR
    - SURFACE CONTROL
36 CENTER STAND PANEL - DAFICS
37 NAV INDICATORS DISPLAY
    MODE SELECT PANEL
38 EMERGENCY GEAR RELEASE HANDLE
39 CENTER CIRCUIT BREAKER PANEL
40 ANNUNCIATOR
41 CENTER STAND PANEL
42 SURFACE LIMITER RELEASE HANDLE
43 MAP PROJECTOR
44 YAW TRIM INDICATOR
45 ROLL TRIM INDICATOR
46 ACCELEROMETER
47 PITCH TRIM INDICATOR
48 FORWARD BYPASS DOOR INDICATOR
49 SPIKE CONTROL PANEL
50 LIQUID OXYGEN QUANTITY INDICATOR
51 DAFICS BIT PANEL
52 PVD CONTROL PANEL
53 ILS CONTROL PANEL
54 VHF CONTROL PANEL
55 IGV AND CABIN PRESSURE PANEL
56 INTERPHONE CONTROL PANEL
57 TACAN CONTROL PANEL
58 AFCS FUNCTION SELECTOR PANEL
59 THROTTLE QUADRANT
60 OXYGEN CONTROL PANEL
61 CANOPY JETTISON HANDLE
62 UHF-1 RADIO CONTROL PANEL
63 FILLER PANEL
64 STANDBY OXYGEN CONTROL PANEL
65 FUEL DERICH AND THROTTLE RESTART CUTOUT PANEL
66 LIGHT CONTROL PANEL
67 EGT AND AFT BYPASS DOOR CONTROL PANEL
68 MAP PROJECTOR CONTROL PANEL
69 ROLL TRIM AND RUDDER SYNC PANEL

M203-9.385(a)

The front cockpit of the SR-71 was completely conventional in appearance, returning to round-dial instruments instead of the more exotic vertical tape instruments used in the YF-12As. The large square instrument below the HSI is a map display, important at the speeds the Blackbirds traveled. (U.S. Air Force)

The Blackbirds used JP-7 fuel that had a special additive to raise the flash point so the fuel would not break down at extreme temperatures. In an emergency situation, crews were authorized to refuel with JP-4 or JP-5, however this limited the aircraft to Mach 1.5 at fairly low altitudes. All 80,280 pounds of JP-7 were carried in six main fuselage tanks and served as a major heat sink for the airframe. Besides cooling the airframe, fuel was used as a cooling medium for other components throughout the aircraft. The aircraft generally took-off with between 45,000 and 65,000 pounds of fuel, and refueled in-flight as necessary to meet mission requirements. It was possible to take-off with a full load of JP-7, but it was not considered practical since fuel leakage, tire and brake heating, abort criteria, and single-engine performance all conspired against the Blackbird with a full load of fuel. Generally, only the flight test aircraft at Palmdale took-off with full tanks since tanker support was more difficult to schedule for them.

The fuel tanks always leaked when cool, and shallow drip pans were

The different shape of the OXCART and SR-71 nose chines shows up here. The A-12 (top) had a much sharper taper than the SR-71 (above). Both aircraft used similar pitot tubes on the nose. These aircraft (60-6924 and 64-17973) are located at Blackbird Air Park in Palmdale, and allow an easy comparison since they are sitting side-by-side. (Dennis R. Jenkins)

The Blackbirds all shared a large double-delta wing planform. Most of the outer skin was corrugated to allow it to absorb the significant thermal-induced growth-contraction caused by skin temperatures that could rise in excess of 600°F. (Lockheed via Tony Landis)

usually placed under the aircraft to capture the leaking JP-7. Maintenance manuals listed the allowable "drips per minute" for each location on the aircraft. Over the years, many different sealants were tried in attempts to stop the leaks but none of them worked particularly well in the extreme environments where the Blackbird flew. Since JP-7 was not particularly flammable at room temperature, it was not much of a safety risk and appropriate safety precautions were developed.

The Blackbirds also used their fuel as hydraulic fluid to actuate certain systems. An engine-driven pump provided 1,800 PSI of recirculated fuel to activate various engine and inlet components, then returned it to be burned. Liquid triethylborane (TEB), which has the physical prop-

The first SR-71B (64-17956) shows the elevated second cockpit used by the instructor pilot. Like the YF-12As, the SR-71 trainers had small ventral fins under the engine nacelles (but not the large central ventral fin). It is interesting to note that the "Titanium Goose" A-12 trainer did not carry the ventral fins, possibly because its J75 engines could not be coaxed to go fast enough for the instability caused by the second cockpit to reveal itself. (Lockheed via Tony Landis)

A single SR-71A (64-17959) was modified to a "Big Tail" configuration during 1974. Operation of the tail was complex since it had to be articulated upward during take-off and landing to avoid being scraped on the runway, but had to quickly be lowered prior to the drag chute being deployed to avoid tangling up the chute risers. This aircraft was retired in 1976, and later put on display at the Armament Museum at Eglin AFB. (Lockheed via Tony Landis)

erty of igniting when exposed to air, was used to ignite the JP-7 for engine start, and to light the afterburner section. A 600cc sealed container on each engine provided 16 metered "shots" to start the engine or ignite the afterburner. Unlike most aircraft, the SR-71 was flown in almost continuous afterburner when not at subsonic speeds. In the event the aircraft ran out of TEB in-flight, the afterburners could be ignited by a catalytic igniter consisting of a ceramic disk and two sets of pure platinum screening disks.

The "Big Tail" SR-71A (64-17959) on display at the Armament Museum at Eglin AFB, Florida. This eight-foot articulated rear fuselage addition was to carry additional reconnaissance equipment, most notably the Optical Bar Camera (OBC) usually carried in the nose. This would have allowed the nose to carry a mapping radar. Another idea was to install real-time satellite data link equipment in the tail. The fuel dump was extended along the top of the "Big Tail" and vented through the flattened tube on the top. The tail was damaged during transport to the museum, and a worker is using automotive "bondo" to fix a mostly titanium aircraft. (Dennis R. Jenkins)

WARBIRD**TECH**
S E R I E S

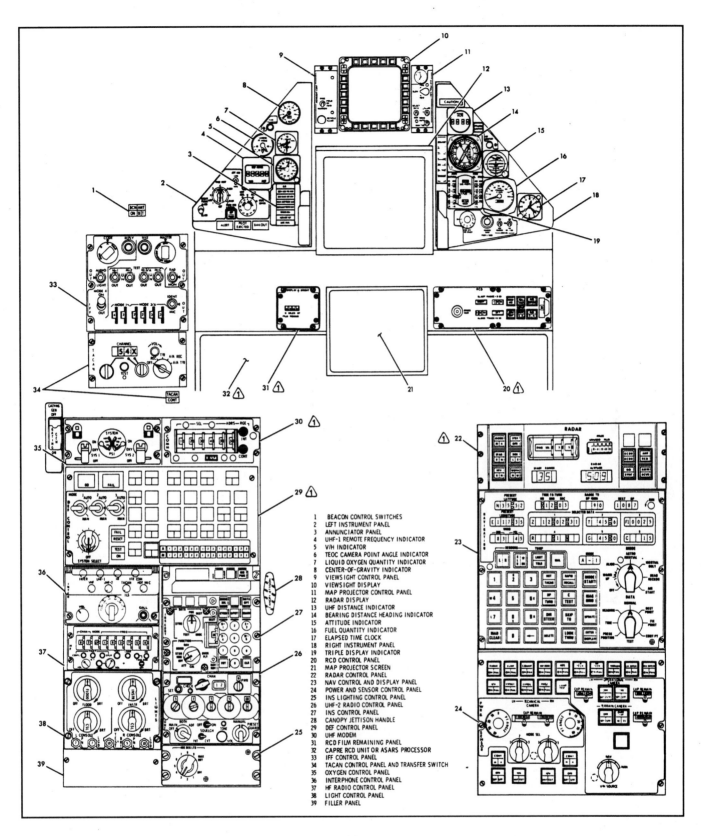

1 BEACON CONTROL SWITCHES
2 LEFT INSTRUMENT PANEL
3 ANNUNCIATOR PANEL
4 UHF-1 REMOTE FREQUENCY INDICATOR
5 V/H INDICATOR
6 TEOC CAMERA POINT ANGLE INDICATOR
7 LIQUID OXYGEN QUANTITY INDICATOR
8 CENTER-OF-GRAVITY INDICATOR
9 VIEWSIGHT CONTROL PANEL
10 VIEWSIGHT DISPLAY
11 MAP PROJECTOR CONTROL PANEL
12 RADAR DISPLAY
13 UHF DISTANCE INDICATOR
14 BEARING DISTANCE HEADING INDICATOR
15 ATTITUDE INDICATOR
16 FUEL QUANTITY INDICATOR
17 ELAPSED TIME CLOCK
18 RIGHT INSTRUMENT PANEL
19 TRIPLE DISPLAY INDICATOR
20 RCD CONTROL PANEL
21 MAP PROJECTOR SCREEN
22 RADAR CONTROL PANEL
23 NAV CONTROL AND DISPLAY PANEL
24 POWER AND SENSOR CONTROL PANEL
25 INS LIGHTING CONTROL PANEL
26 UHF-2 RADIO CONTROL PANEL
27 INS CONTROL PANEL
28 CANOPY JETTISON HANDLE
29 DEF CONTROL PANEL
30 UHF MODEM
31 RCD FILM REMAINING PANEL
32 CAPRE RCD UNIT OR ASARS PROCESSOR
33 IFF CONTROL PANEL
34 TACAN CONTROL PANEL AND TRANSFER SWITCH
35 OXYGEN CONTROL PANEL
36 INTERPHONE CONTROL PANEL
37 HF RADIO CONTROL PANEL
38 LIGHT CONTROL PANEL
39 FILLER PANEL

The SR-71 aft cockpit contained the controls and monitors for the reconnaissance equipment as well as the defense electronics (ECM). Almost half of the left console was devoted to ECM controls. The three screens in the center of the instrument panel are, from top to bottom: the view sight display; the radar display; and the map projection screen. The back seater was also responsible for navigation, and the center portion of the right console is devoted to navigation equipment. (U.S. Air Force)

The first flight of the "Big Tail" SR-71A (64-17959) was on 3 December 1974, and its last flight was not quite two years later on 29 October 1976. With the war in Vietnam over, and budgets tight, the Air Force elected not to pursue a conversion program for additional aircraft. The aircraft had only 866.1 flight hours when it was permanently retired. (Lockheed via Tony Landis)

The large intake spikes were one of the last items installed on the aircraft on the final assembly line. The spikes are standing vertically behind this SR-71A. Small parts of the aircraft were built-up in the area behind the final assembly line. (Lockheed via Tony Landis)

Two 106 liter dewars of liquid nitrogen in the nose wheel well were used to purge the fuel tanks as they emptied. Without the nitrogen purge the aircraft was limited to Mach 2.6 to prevent autogenous ignition of the ullage vapors. Late in their career, an additional 50 liter dewar was added to some SR-71s to allow longer missions.

The basic Pratt & Whitney J58 engine was 20 feet long, 4.5 feet in diameter and weighed 6,500 pounds. Early engines provided approximately 30,000 pounds-thrust, while later engines were uprated to almost 34,000 LBF. Most documentation does not differentiate between the engines and simply lists them as 32,000 LBF. By comparison, each engine produced more horsepower than the Queen Mary ocean liner. Each hour of maximum thrust at sea level consumed 65,000 pounds of JP-7 and 1,173,600 pounds of air. Fortunately, Mach 3 flight was more econom-

The forward part of each engine nacelle was fixed and did not swing upward with the outer wing panels. However, enough of the nacelle opened to completely access the J58 engine. Maintenance on the various inlet ramps and vents was accomplished by removing smaller panels around the nacelle. (Lockheed via Tony Landis)

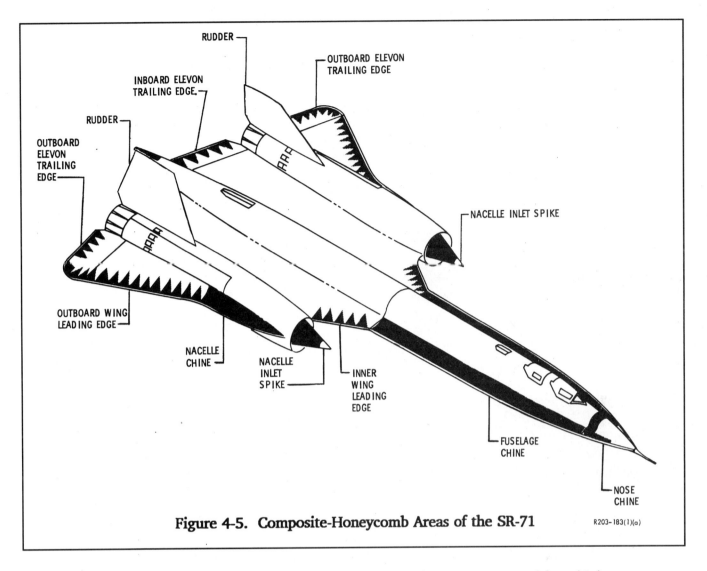

RUDDER

INBOARD ELEVON
TRAILING EDGE

OUTBOARD ELEVON
TRAILING EDGE

RUDDER

OUTBOARD
ELEVON
TRAILING
EDGE

NACELLE INLET SPIKE

OUTBOARD WING
LEADING EDGE

NACELLE
CHINE

NACELLE
INLET
SPIKE

INNER
WING
LEADING
EDGE

FUSELAGE
CHINE

NOSE
CHINE

R203–183(1)(a)

Figure 4-5. Composite-Honeycomb Areas of the SR-71

Almost all of the chines and wing leading edges of the Blackbirds were constructed from high-temperature composite material. On some aircraft the rudders were also composite, although the SR-71 usually used all-metal rudders. (U.S. Air Force)

ical, consuming only 11,000 pounds of JP-7. At maximum operating temperature, the engine would grow six inches in length and 2.5 inches in diameter, while using 800°F air to cool itself.

Starting the engines required an external starting system consisting of two automotive V-8 engines in a special "Buick" cart. Originally these were Buick engines, hence the name, but later were replaced by big-block Chevys. The engines drove a geared vertical shaft that connected to the bottom of the J58

and spun the turbines. These special carts were developed since there were no air starting carts (the more normal method) when the Blackbird first entered service capable of supplying sufficient volume to rotate the engines. The J58 used special lubricants that were particularly thick at room temperature and had to be preheated to 158°F before the engine could be rotated in any case. The YF-12A developed a cartridge-start system, although it was not adapted for operational use. Eventually, air-start systems were developed that could rotate a

J58 and each of the SR-71 shelters at Beale and Kadena were equipped with these, all but eliminating the "Buick" starting carts.

At its Mach 3.2 cruise speed, approximately 20% of total thrust was produced by the Blackbird engine's turbine section. The remaining thrust was provided by a combination of the nacelle and the afterburner (non-turbine) section of the engine. Each nacelle had six 9-inch diameter bypass tubes running along the sides of the engine, and at high Mach speeds, a large por-

The large all-flying rudders rotated around a single pivot and looked very fragile (they were not). Two different types of rudders were used on the Blackbirds: an all metal unit, and a high-temperature plastic composite unit. Most A-12s spent their careers with the composite units, while the SR-71s used metal rudders most of the time. The rudders were interchangeable between all the Blackbirds. (Lockheed via Tony Landis)

tion of the air was bypassed around the compressor and turbine sections through these tubes directly into the afterburner section. This bypass air was mixed with raw fuel and ignited (typical of most afterburners), providing a significant increase in available thrust. unlike most jet engines however, the J58 was designed to run in almost continuous afterburner. This high-percentage of bypassed air is why some sources have called the J58 a turbo-ramjet engine. Although this is technically not totally correct, conceptually it describes the operation of the Blackbird's propulsion system quite well.

Each inlet was characterized by a large spike that was positioned full forward at subsonic speeds and moved by a large hydraulic actuator over a range of 26 inches. As the aircraft approached Mach 1.6 and 30,000 feet, the spikes unlocked and moved aft approximately 1.825 inches for each 0.1 Mach. As each spike moved slowly aft, their conical shape increased the captured air stream area by up to 112% and reduced the throat area by 54 percent. A series of bypass doors, centerbody bleed vents, and slots around the inlet controlled the pressure and speed of air flowing through and around the engine. At low speeds (mainly for take-off), there was no surplus air available to be bypassed around the turbine section into the afterburner, leading to a series of 'suck-in' doors being opened to provide fresh air to the afterburner. By Mach 0.5 these doors had closed and bypass air was diverted through the inlet and around the turbine section to the afterburner.

The operation of all the vents and doors, except for the aft bypass doors, were controlled by the Air Inlet Computer (AIC). The aft bypass doors were always under the manual control of the pilot. Col. Richard Graham gives an excellent description of the inlet operations in *SR-71 Revealed: The Inside Story*.

One of the more interesting aspects of the inlet operations was the concept of "unstarts." An "unstart" refers to a phenomenon of supersonic inlets when the compressor inlet pressure becomes too

One of the most famous pieces of tail art that adorned the SR-71 was "Rapid Rabbit" (64-17978). This SR-71 was used extensive for surveillance over North Vietnam while based at Kadena. The Playboy™ bunny was white, and apparently used with the implicit (if not explicit) permission of Hugh Hefner. (Lockheed via the Mick Roth Collection)

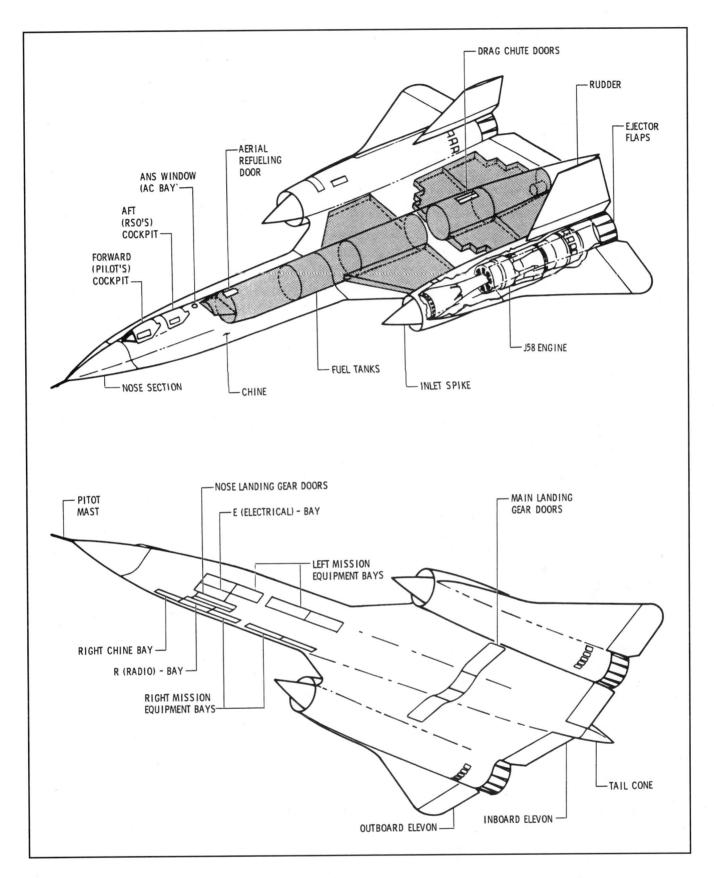

DRAG CHUTE DOORS

RUDDER

EJECTOR FLAPS

AERIAL REFUELING DOOR

ANS WINDOW (AC BAY)

AFT (RSO'S) COCKPIT

FORWARD (PILOT'S) COCKPIT

J58 ENGINE

FUEL TANKS

INLET SPIKE

NOSE SECTION

CHINE

NOSE LANDING GEAR DOORS

E (ELECTRICAL) - BAY

MAIN LANDING GEAR DOORS

PITOT MAST

LEFT MISSION EQUIPMENT BAYS

RIGHT CHINE BAY

R (RADIO) - BAY

RIGHT MISSION EQUIPMENT BAYS

TAIL CONE

OUTBOARD ELEVON

INBOARD ELEVON

Although a large aircraft, the SR-71 had remarkably little internal space. This was largely because almost the entire fuselage was taken up with six large fuel tanks. The nose area contained the crew and most mission equipment. The outer wing panels did not contain anything except actuators for the outer elevons. (U.S. Air Force)

VX-4 at Pt. Mugu has traditionally had a black aircraft … for years an F-4 (shown here) and later an F-14. The SR-71A (64-17955) was the test and evaluation unit based at Plant 42 in Palmdale. Very early in their careers the SR-71s carried the last three of their serial number on the forward nacelles as "buzz numbers." (Mick Roth Collection)

A tire failed during take-off, resulting in this SR-71A (64-17977) running off the end of the runway at Beale AFB on 10 October 1968. The RSO, Maj. James Kogler ejected, but the pilot, Maj. Gabriel Kardong stayed with the aircraft. Both officers were unhurt in the incident but the aircraft was severely damaged by the ensuing fire and was written-off. Notice that the rear canopy is missing, while the front canopy is open. (U.S. Air Force via the Mick Roth Collection)

great and has no place to go inside the inlet and therefore unstarts in order to relieve the excess pressure building up. An unstart was recognized in the cockpit by a loud "BANG" accompanied by the aircraft yawing and pitching violently. It should be noted that the J58 continued to operate normally through an unstart, although the afterburner might go out. After a few disconcerting adventures with unstarts, Lockheed devised a system that caused the second inlet to sympathetically go through the same restart cycle. This effectively reduced the violent yaw and pitching movements of the aircraft, although it still presented the pilot with an unpleasant, and potentially dangerous, experience.

Maintenance on the Blackbirds presented some interesting challenges of their own. The hydraulic systems were designed to withstand the tremendous heat generated by Mach 3 flight. Unfortunately, many of the problems reported by the flight crews only manifested themselves at these high temperatures. Special carts were devised that heated the aircraft's hydraulic fluid to in-flight temperatures to allow ground maintenance crews to duplicate problems.

During the late 1970s a significant upgrade program for the SR-71 was developed under project SENIOR KING. At a cost of $10 million per aircraft, each SR-71 would have been equipped with modern computers, digital signal processing capabilities, and a long conformal antenna running down the top of the fuselage that provided a satellite data link directly to commanders in the field or the National Command Authority. This would have eliminated the SR-71's largest

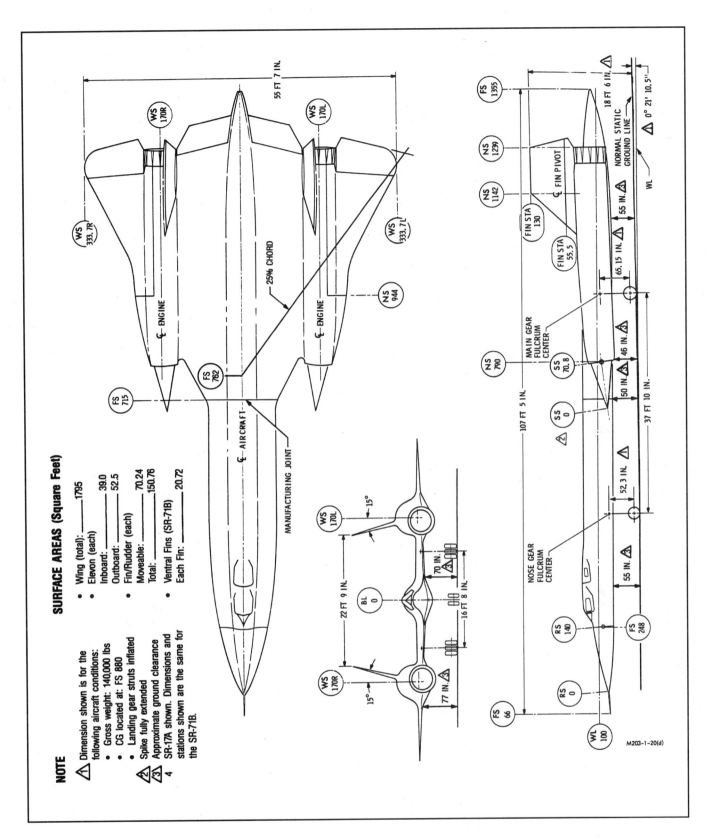

The manufacturing joint at fuselage station 715 (FS715) provided a convenient place to take the Blackbirds apart when they began to be shipped to museums around the country. Unfortunately, the aft fuselage and wing did not present such a convenient location and most Blackbirds had their wing structures cut so that they could be transported by road without the hassles and restrictions that confronted Lockheed when they were originally transported from Burbank. This ensures most of the aircraft will never return to flight status. (U.S. Air Force)

drawback, the fact that the aircraft had to return to base before its intelligence data could be downloaded and disseminated. Unfortunately SENIOR KING was not funded and never progressed further than the prototype stage. Later tests also used an antenna mounted under the aircraft to allow data to be transmitted directly to ground stations. This modification was also not funded.

There was only one significant external modification to the SR-71A during its service career, and this was made to only a single aircraft (64-17959). The "Big Tail" modification was an attempt to increase the payload capacity of the SR-71. Numerous studies were made to determine a method of providing additional sensor capabilities to the aircraft without a major remanufacturing effort. Because the internal volume of the aircraft was small since most of the fuselage was used by the fuel tank, most concepts involved the use of external pods for ECM and SIGINT equipment. This would have had a slightly adverse effect on the speed and range of the SR-71, but was considered the most likely concept until somebody suggested an eight-foot extension of the aft fuselage.

One disadvantage of this concept was that the entire assembly would need to be articulated to clear the runway during take-off and landing, but it also offered an additional way to trim the aircraft while in-flight. The assembly could be moved up and down over a range of 8.5° on either side of center to accommodate the high angle-of-attack used by the Blackbird during take-offs and landings. On landing approach, the extension was moved to the fully up position and as the wheels touched down the extension was moved to the fully down position so as not to interfere with the deployment of the chute.

Housed inside the movable "Big Tail" were various combinations of sensors and other equipment including a future satellite data link antenna in the tail to allow real-time transmission of reconnaissance data. The first flight of the Big Tail configuration was on 3 December 1974 and the last flight was on 29 October 1976. Declining budgets and the end of the Vietnam conflict caused the Air Force to cancel the expected production program. With only 866.1 hours on the airframe, the Big Tail was stricken from the inventory and placed in non-flyable storage at Plant 42. In late 1991 the aircraft was disassembled and transported by road to the Armament Museum outside Eglin AFB, Florida.

The Pratt & Whitney J58 was 20 feet long, 4.5 feet in diameter, and weighed 6,500 pounds. Early versions produced approximately 30,000 pounds-thrust although later versions produced as much as 34,000 pounds-thrust. The engine operated in continuous afterburner during cruise and consumed over 11,000 pounds of JP-7 fuel per hour. The engine inlet had to be capable of withstanding temperatures in excess of 800°F under some conditions. Inlet fuel temperatures could reach 300°F and the fuel at the afterburner injectors was 700°F. Lubricating oil would vary between 700°F to 1,000°F in localized parts of the engine. (Dennis R. Jenkins)

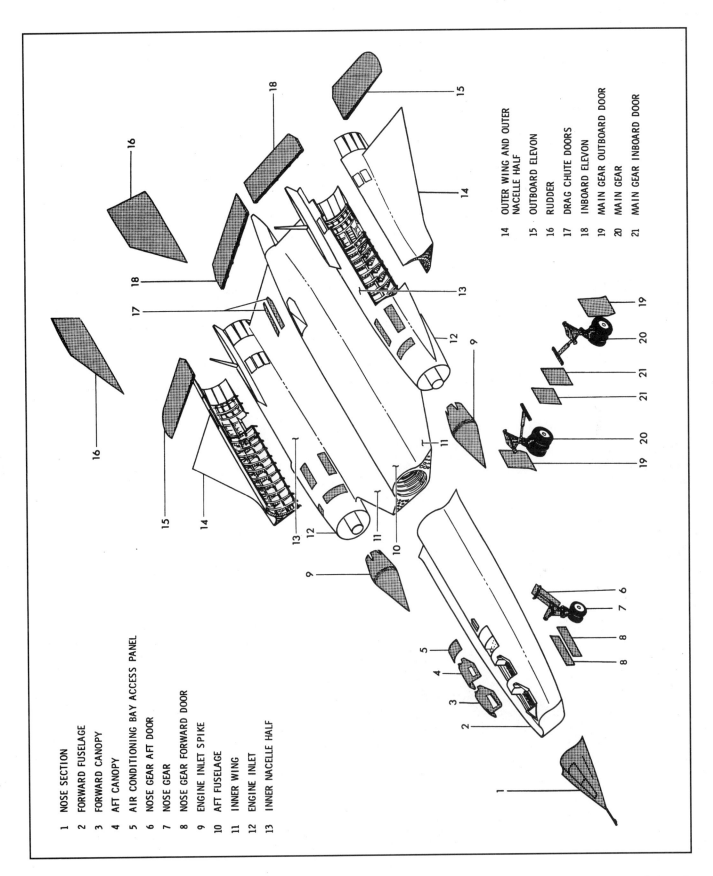

1 NOSE SECTION
2 FORWARD FUSELAGE
3 FORWARD CANOPY
4 AFT CANOPY
5 AIR CONDITIONING BAY ACCESS PANEL
6 NOSE GEAR AFT DOOR
7 NOSE GEAR
8 NOSE GEAR FORWARD DOOR
9 ENGINE INLET SPIKE
10 AFT FUSELAGE
11 INNER WING
12 ENGINE INLET
13 INNER NACELLE HALF

14 OUTER WING AND OUTER
   NACELLE HALF
15 OUTBOARD ELEVON
16 RUDDER
17 DRAG CHUTE DOORS
18 INBOARD ELEVON
19 MAIN GEAR OUTBOARD DOOR
20 MAIN GEAR
21 MAIN GEAR INBOARD DOOR

The Blackbirds were manufactured in essentially two major subassemblies – the forward fuselage; and the aft fuselage and wings. This presented some unique transportation problems when Lockheed moved the aircraft from Burbank to either Groom Lake or Palmdale for their flight tests. (U.S. Air Force)

BYE, BYE, BLACKBIRDS

BROUGHT DOWN BY BOB, NOT SAM

During November 1965, the very month when OXCART was declared operational, the first moves toward its demise commenced. The Bureau of the Budget (BoB) questioned the requirement for both the CIA and Air Force to operate different fleets of seemingly identical aircraft. The fact that the A-12 and the SR-71 were actually substantially different in their capabilities was either overlooked or ignored by the Budget office.

The SR-71 could not match the photographic coverage that the A-12 could provide since its main camera system could only photograph a swath 28 miles wide with a resolution of 28 to 30 inches. The A-12's camera could photograph a swath 72 miles wide with a nadir resolution of 12 to 18 inches and oblique resolution of 54 inches. Thus the A-12's camera covered three times as much territory as the SR-71's, and did so with better resolution. In addition, the A-12 could fly 2,000 to 5,000 feet higher than the SR-71 and was faster, with an operational speed of almost Mach 3.3 compared to the SR-71's Mach 3.1.

In spite of this data, the Bureau of the Budget submitted a memorandum to President Johnson recommending terminating OXCART. On 28 December 1966, the President approved the termination of OXCART by 1 January 1968. The CIA informed the Department of Defense on 10 January 1967 that the A-12's would gradually be placed in storage, with the process to be completed by the end of January 1968.

All of this happened before the OXCART had conducted a single operational mission, which did not occur until 31 May 1967. In the months that followed the OXCART demonstrated its exceptional technical capabilities in operations over Southeast Asia. A few high-level Presidential advisors and Congressional leaders began to question the decision to phase out OXCART.

The CIA contended that the A-12 was the better aircraft because it flew higher, faster, and had superior cameras. The Air Force maintained that its two-seat SR-71 had a better overall suite of equipment, with three different cameras (area search, spotting, and mapping), infrared sensors, side-looking radar, and ELINT-collection gear. In an effort to resolve this argument, the two aircraft were pitted against each other in a fly-off code named NICE GIRL. On 3 November 1967, an A-12 and an SR-71 flew identical flight paths, separated in time by an hour, from north to south roughly above the Mississippi River. The data collected during these missions were evaluated by representatives of the CIA, DIA, and other Department of Defense intelligence organizations.

The results proved inconclusive since both photographic systems provided imagery of sufficient

The surviving M-21(60-6940) and a TAGBOARD drone are on display at the Seattle Museum of Flight. The aircraft have been meticulously restored, and the only disappointment is that the rudders appear to be reproductions. The drone is still in the D-21B configuration with the large air data tubes on each wing. (Troy Downen)

WARBIRDTECH
SERIES

quality for analysis. The A-12's photographic coverage was superior to the SR-71's, but the infrared, side-looking radar, and ELINT equipment provided some unique intelligence not available from the A-12.

Although the fly-off had not settled the question of which aircraft was superior, OXCART did win a temporary reprieve in late November 1967. The Johnson administration decided to keep both fleets since OXCART was actually flying missions over North Vietnam. In the spring of 1968 there was yet another termination study, and on 16 May 1968 the original decision to terminate the OXCART program was reaffirmed. President Johnson concurred on 21 May.

Early in March 1968, SR-71s began to arrive at Kadena to take over the BLACK SHIELD commitment, and the last operational mission flown by OXCART was on 8 May 1968 over North Korea. Several days later the last two A-12s departed Okinawa to join the eight OXCART aircraft already in storage at Palmdale. Because the A-12s were physically different from the SR-71, the only significant parts that could be used to support SENIOR CROWN were the J58 engines. The OXCART's outstanding Perkin-Elmer camera could not be used in the SR-71 because the two-seater Air Force aircraft had a smaller camera compartment than that of the A-12.

The SR-71 would enjoy a long uninterrupted service career after the OXCART was retired. But by the mid-1980s there was increasing pressure to retire the last of the Blackbirds. The most common official reason given was that the aircraft was getting too old to maintain and was too expensive to oper-

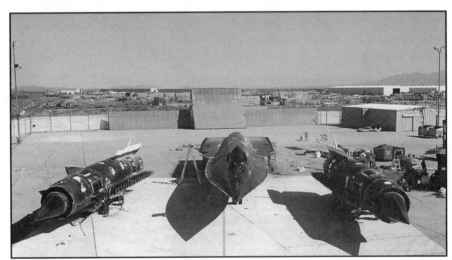

Several of the Blackbirds were transported to their museums by Lockheed C-5 Galaxy transports. This A-12 shows how the wings were cut to allow it to fit into the C-5. (Tony Landis Collection)

ate. The popular reasoning was that satellites could perform strategic reconnaissance faster and cheaper. Amongst the general public it was widely believed that the Blackbird was being retired because a superior replacement ("Aurora"?) was entering service, although there is still no evidence of such a vehicle.

The Strategic Air Command (SAC) operated the SR-71s as well as all US nuclear bombers and tanker assets. General John Chain was the Commander in Chief of SAC and directly responsible for allocating the funding needed to keep the various programs running. General Chain saw redirecting the annual SR-71 budget as a way of continuing to fund the cost overruns being experienced on the B-1B bomber program, as well as modernizing the ICBM fleet. General Larry Welch,

Blackbird Air Park at Air Force Plant 42 in Palmdale, California, is the only place you can see an A-12 and an SR-71 on display side-by-side. This seems fitting since the museum is only a couple of miles away from the "Skunk Works" new location at Site 10 and the old Blackbird modification center at Site 2. (Tony Landis)

head of the Air Force's Programs and Resources directorate concurred, believing that the SR-71 was "… too expensive, vulnerable to enemy defenses, and duplicated overhead systems."

At the time of its retirement, the SR-71 was not suffering from any fatigue problems. In fact, because of the temperature cycles it went through on each mission, the airframe was actually stronger than it had ever been due to an annealing process. However, the SR-71 was fairly expensive to operate, costing approximately $300 million annually. This included two detachments of 13-15 SR-71s and their dedicated tanker support. Proposals had been circulated that reduced the operational SR-71 fleet to five aircraft that could be operated for as little as $150 million annually. Other "bare-bones" scenarios cost under $100 million annually.

The Air Force did have one very legitimate complaint against the aircraft. The largest users of the SR-71 were the CIA, the State Department, and the Navy. Interesting, the Air Force did not get to choose most of the missions that were flown by the SR-71. These decisions were made by the National Reconnaissance Office (NRO) or the Office of the Secretary of Defense. However, funding for the SR-71 came out of Air Force's budget, where it competed with other programs of more importance to Air Force management. There had been proposals to treat the SR-71 as a national asset and fund it accordingly, but this never materialized.

The FY90 defense appropriations request did not contain funding for the SR-71. A great deal of lobbying occurred on each side of the debate, but in the end, no funds were forthcoming. Operational training sorties were flown right until the end, with the last one occurring on 7 November 1989 flown by LtCol. Tom McCleary and LtCol. Stan Gudmundson. This final sortie took place exactly 21 years, 7 months, and 17 days after the first SR-71 operational sortie.

Even the actual retirement of the SR-71 demonstrated its unpopularity with Air Force management. Usually aircraft are maintained in storage for some period of time in case a need is discovered for its reuse. An obvious example of this is the storage of the A-12s and D-21s earlier in the Blackbird's career. However, the SR-71's were almost immediately disassembled and shipped to museums around the country. In many cases this disassembly involved cutting significant structural pieces, ensuring the aircraft could never return to flight status.

On 6 March 1990, nearly two months after the SR-71 was officially retired from the Air Force, an SR-71A (64-17972) set four international speed records while being delivered to the Smithsonian National Air and Space Museum at Dulles International Airport, Washington, D.C. The aircraft was flown by LtCol. Ed Yeilding and LtCol. Joseph T. "JT" Vida and flew coast-to-coast (2,404 miles) in 67 minutes and 54 seconds, averaging 2,124 MPH.

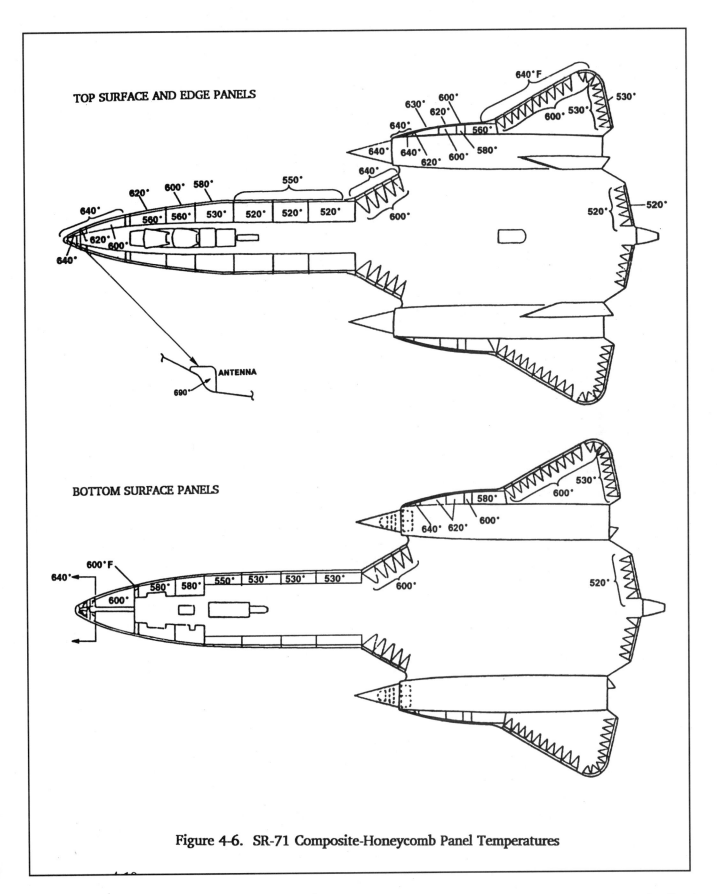

TOP SURFACE AND EDGE PANELS

ANTENNA

BOTTOM SURFACE PANELS

Figure 4-6. SR-71 Composite-Honeycomb Panel Temperatures

Except for the first A-12 all the Blackbirds used high-temperature plastic composite for the chines and wing leading edges. The composite had to withstand temperatures in excess of 600°F in some regions. (U.S. Air Force)

RESURRECTION

Ironically, less than a year after the SR-71s were retired it became apparent just how wrong this decision was. When Operation DESERT SHIELD began, Gen. Norman Schwarzkopf was reported to have asked for SR-71s to be reactivated for use in gathering near-real time reconnaissance. The Air Force asked Skunk Works how long it would take to reactivate one or more of the SR-71As in storage at Plant 42. Lockheed

responded that a single aircraft could be operational within two weeks and a second aircraft 30 days later. Lockheed figured they could scrounge sufficient equipment for the first aircraft by cannibalizing other stored aircraft and the additional time for the second aircraft was necessary to locate equipment that had been dispersed when the fleet was retired. The Air Force declined the opportunity.

On 19 September 1994 Congress passed the FY95 defense authorization bill and added $100 million to bring three SR-71s out of storage. The Air Force continued to state that it did not want the aircraft and refused to allocate the money to be spent. Nevertheless, the Air Force did ask former Habu crews still on active duty if they would like to volunteer to fly the reactivated aircraft, and on 29 January 1995 three crews were selected to fly the aircraft. Eventually, bowing to Congressional pressure, the Air Force authorized the reactivation program.

On 26 April 1995 the first of the reactivated SR-71As (64-17971) flew its first sortie with a NASA crew at the controls. This aircraft had been used by NASA since its original Air Force retirement as NASA 832, and had been completely refurbished by Lockheed in Palmdale. The second reactivated SR-71A (64-17967)

(Above) After they were reactivated, the two Air Force SR-71As (64-17967 and 64-17971) were based at Edwards AFB in order to share support services, simulators, and the SR-71B (64-17956) with NASA's Dryden Flight Research Center. The Edwards main base and runways are visible below. (Lockheed)

The first reactivated Air Force SR-71 (64-17971) initially carried unique markings with a "BB" tail code in red above the serial number. The aircraft later reverted back to a simple serial number as was previously used. (Tony Landis Collection)

The SR-71s carry markings very similar to those used just before they were retired. The aircraft have been completely refurbished and should have a long useful life ahead of them. The aircraft were stripped down to their airframes, fuel tanks stripped and resealed, and some avionics updated. Various improvements to their mission equipment, such as satellite data links, are also expected to be installed. (Lockheed)

made its first flight on 28 August 1995. Both aircraft have been equipped with a satellite data link to provide near-real-time transmission of intelligence data. The Air Force aircraft are based in a renovated hanger at Edwards AFB. Interesting, this is the last Air Force hanger on the flight line before you get to the Dryden Flight Research Center, which operates the other two flyable SR-71s. The original government estimate for reactivating and updating two aircraft was $100 million. The final cost ended up being somewhat less than $72 million, another tribute to Skunk Works when they want to save money.

Estimated operational costs are $40 million per year, not including tanker support, and Congress is now funding the SR-71 as a separate line item, so it doesn't compete with any specific military program. Further, the newly created Defense Airborne Reconnaissance Office (DARO) has a vested interest in airborne systems, so suddenly there's a constituency to lobby for the SR-71. In addition, the SR-71 is going to be operated more in a tactical role, so it isn't competing directly with the satellites.

SR-71s WITH NASA

Throughout 1989 and 1990, as the rumors of terminating the SR-71 program were getting stronger, NASA began to express an interest in obtaining several Blackbirds to continue the high-speed research that had been terminated during the late 1970s when the YF-12s were retired. Negotiations led to NASA receiving permission to use two SR-71As (64-17971 and 17980) that were in storage at Beale AFB, as well as the SR-71B trainer that had been undergoing major overhaul in Palmdale when the program was terminated. Also included in the deal was a new $22 million simulator that had been ordered from Singer-Link in 1988. The SR-71B (844, 64-17956) is shared by Dryden and Air Force pilots as needed and the second SR-71A (832, 64-17971) was subsequently returned to the Air Force to become the first aircraft reactivated for Air Force reconnaissance missions.

LtCol. Rod Dyckman (retired) took a leave of absence from American Airlines to fly the Functional Check Flight on the newly overhauled trainer. He also flew two additional

The NASA SR-71A (64-17980) being repainted after it was refurbished. This aircraft had less than five flight hours since its last major overhaul before it was placed in storage. (Lockheed)

In full afterburner the Blackbirds trailed over twenty feet of flame and diamond-shaped shock cones. This is NASA's SR-71A (64-17980) taking off from Edwards AFB. (NASA / Dryden)

In 1990 this SR-71 (64-19780) was used briefly by Pratt & Whitney for a test program. Noteworthy is the P&W logo on the vertical stabilizer. The red 40-foot diameter drag chute is used on every full-stop landing. (NASA / Dryden)

flights to check out NASA test pilot Steve Ishmael, who in turn would check out other NASA pilots. Surprisingly, many retired Air Force and Lockheed personnel volunteered their services to assist NASA in making the three SR-71s operational.

The SR-71's operating environment makes the aircraft an excellent platform to carry out research and experiments in a variety of areas – aerodynamics, propulsion, structures, thermal protection materials, high-speed and high-temperature instrumentation, atmospheric studies and sonic boom characterization.

One of the first major experiments to be flown in the NASA SR-71 program was a laser air data collection system. The system used six beams

The SR-71B trainer (64-17956) is operated by NASA's Dryden Flight Research Center, but it is also used by the Air Force as required to support their operational Blackbirds. Neither organization could probably afford to operate the aircraft by itself, so this sharing arrangement is beneficial to both. The raised second cockpit and ventral fins under the engine nacelles are visible. (NASA / Dryden)

Studies at NASA Dryden have shown external payloads could be carried both above and below the SR-71. The upper mounting location has been well researched as part of the D/M-21 program, and will be used for the LASRE program. The lower location has had some flight experience in the COLD WALL experiment on the YF-12A. (NASA /DFRC)

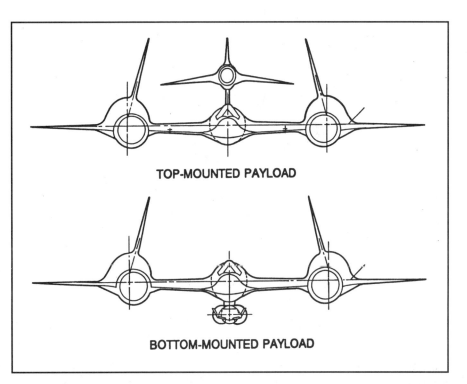

TOP-MOUNTED PAYLOAD

BOTTOM-MOUNTED PAYLOAD

of laser light projected from the bottom of NASA's SR-71A. As microscopic-size atmospheric particles passed between the beams, direction and speed were measured and processed into standard speed and attitude references. This provided a non-mechanical alternative to the normal air-pressure derived pitot-static systems currently used on most aircraft.

The first of a series of flights using the SR-71 as a science camera platform was flown in March 1993 for NASA's Jet Propulsion Laboratory. An upward-looking ultraviolet video camera mounted in a modified nose compartment studied a variety of celestial objects in wavelengths that are blocked to ground-based astronomers.

Both of the NASA SR-71s carry a white NASA strip with the red NASA in it. The SR-71B is fully capable of conducting NASA research missions, with only slightly less internal volume for experiment equipment. (NASA / Dryden)

The SR-71 has also been used to assist in the development of the IRIDIUM satellite-based instant wireless personal communications network being developed by Motorola's Satellite Communications Division. During the development tests, the SR-71 acted as a "surrogate satellite" for transmitters and receivers on the ground.

The Blackbirds, like most delta wing aircraft, have a fairly high angle-of-attack on take off and landing. Here the NASA SR-71A (64-17980) is shown at Edwards AFB. (NASA /Dryden)

When the SR-71s were retired, three (64-17956, 17971, and 17980) of them were assigned to future use at NASA. Here they pose for a family portrait with the trainer (64-17956) in the middle during 1992. (NASA / Dryden)

The SR-71 has also been used in a program to study ways of reducing sonic boom overpressures that are heard on the ground. Data from the Sonic Boom Mitigation Study could eventually lead to aircraft designs that would reduce the "peak" of sonic booms and minimize the affect they produce on the ground. This is a continuation of research begun with the YF-12A and XB-70 20 years earlier.

For a short time in 1994 NASA used a second SR-71A (64-17971) and assigned it the number 832. This aircraft was later transferred back to the Air Force. (NASA / Dryden)

The Linear Aerospike SR-71 Experiment (LASRE) is designed to flight test a linear aerospike rocket engine mounted on a 10%-scale, half-span model of Lockheed Martin's X-33 technology demonstrator. Following ground testing of the engine at the Air Force's Phillips Laboratory at Edwards AFB, the LASRE will be mounted and flown piggyback on NASA's SR-71A (844, 64-17980) during the summer of 1997. Linear aerospike rocket engines have been laboratory and ground tested many times over the past thirty years, but have never actually flown.

The aerospike engine and half-span scale model are mounted on top of

The SR-71B trainer (64-17956) is fully capable of being refueled like all Blackbirds. The Air Force provides the tanker resources for all Dryden flight research missions that require refueling. This includes most Blackbird missions, although NASA does fly some research flights that only use internal fuel. (NASA/Dryden)

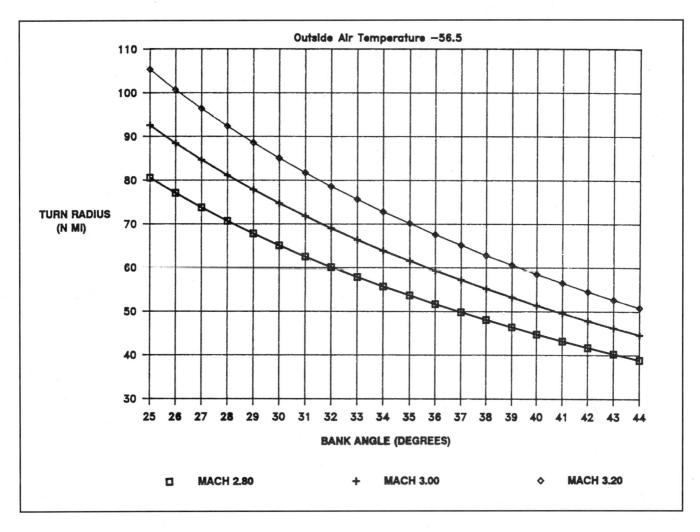

Outside Air Temperature −56.5

TURN RADIUS (N MI) vs BANK ANGLE (DEGREES)

□ MACH 2.80   + MACH 3.00   ◇ MACH 3.20

Turning at Mach 3 takes some room. With a shallow bank angle (recommended) it can take over 100 miles for the Blackbirds to make a turn. This chart lists the amount of distance required to turn at various bank angles at the most common operational speeds. (NASA/DFRC)

the SR-71A in a "canoe" which contains propellant tanks and instrumentation gear. The assembly is 41 feet long, weighs 13,800 pounds, and is mounted in roughly the same position as the D-21 drone pylon used by the M-21. Thirteen flight tests will measure the rocket engine's performance, from subsonic speeds up to Mach 3. The aerospike engine is expected to produce 7,000 LBF at Mach 3. The

The SR-71B (64-17956) backs off from a tanker after refueling in December 1994. JP-7 can be seen leaking on the upper wing surfaces. (NASA / Dryden)

NASA almost always sends a chase aircraft along with the SR-71 flights, although they obviously can not keep up with the Blackbird during the high-speed portions of flight. Here an F/A-18 Hornet flies chase on the SR-71B (64-17956). (NASA/Dryden)

total cost of the LASRE program is approximately $14 million.

Linear aerospike rocket engines have been around for over thirty years and is very similar to normal rocket engines in it's plumbing and accessories, utilizing similar components, such as turbopumps. The most notable difference is the absence of a bell-shaped nozzle. The linear aerospike engine uses the atmosphere as part of it's nozzle, with the surrounding airflow containing the rocket's exhaust plume. This keeps the engine at optimum performance and efficiency at all altitudes during ascent to orbit. Another advantage is that linear aerospike engines are 75% smaller than bell-nozzle rocket engines of comparable thrust. The smaller design means less engine weight and less engine support structure required, which allows for lighter spacecraft.

Only now is the performance potential of the Blackbird becoming well understood. The SR-71 was intended for flight at altitudes

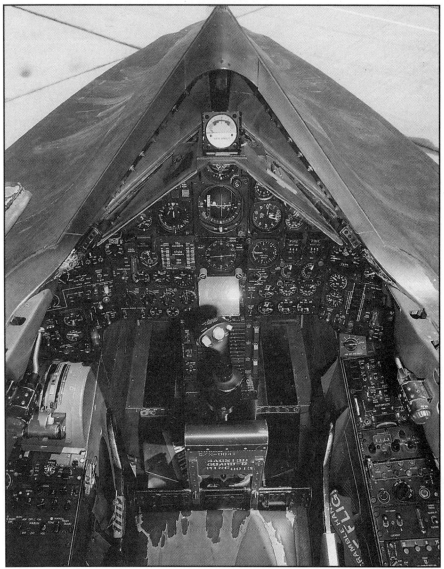

The front cockpit of this NASA SR-71A (64-17980) is virtually identical to how it appeared in Air Force service (most of the sensitive items were in the back cockpit). The cockpit is fairly roomy appearing, but remember that the flight crew wears full pressure suits, making the accommodations rather tight for most pilots. (Tony Landis)

All of the Blackbird series had an air data probe on the extreme nose which was the only location on the aircraft that had undisturbed air. Later in their careers many SR-71s used additional pitot tubes located on the forward fuselage as secondary inputs for their Digital Automatic Flight and Inlet Control System (DAFICS) that replaced the original analog Automatic Flight Control System (AFCS). (U.S. Air Force)

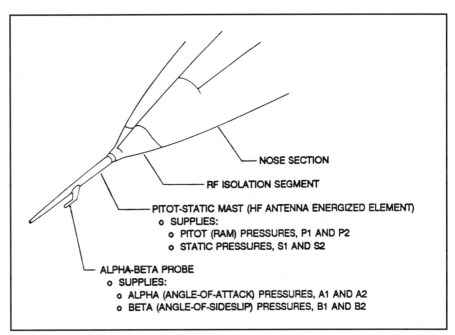

NOSE SECTION

RF ISOLATION SEGMENT

PITOT-STATIC MAST (HF ANTENNA ENERGIZED ELEMENT)
o SUPPLIES:
o PITOT (RAM) PRESSURES, P1 AND P2
o STATIC PRESSURES, S1 AND S2

ALPHA-BETA PROBE
o SUPPLIES:
o ALPHA (ANGLE-OF-ATTACK) PRESSURES, A1 AND A2
o BETA (ANGLE-OF-SIDESLIP) PRESSURES, B1 AND B2

approaching 85,000 feet, with sustained cruising speeds approaching Mach 3.2 – the smaller and lighter A-12 could better each of these by a small margin. During its operational career, the SR-71 rarely exceeded these design speed or altitude limits. Studies have been conducted by Lockheed and NASA that show speeds in excess of Mach 3.5 could be attained for 10-15 minutes. The studies indicated that increasing the maximum speed to Mach 3.4 would not require any significant modifications to the aircraft, but for sustained flight between Mach 3.4 and Mach 3.5, the inlet hydraulic lines and actuators would need to be better insulated to protect them from the additional heat. NASA had planned to conduct an envelope expansion program for the SR-71, but ever tightening budgets led to these plans being cancelled in the early 1990s. The only structural limitation related to speed above Mach 3.5 is an absolute limit of 420 Knots Equivalent Air Speed (KEAS), set by inlet duct pressures and temperatures which exceed acceptable values. Other factors which limit speed above Mach 3.5 are inlet capture area and excessive engine compressor inlet temperature (CIT).

One of the NASA studies also addressed achieving higher altitude

flight. The results indicated that a "zoom climb" profile would allow reaching 95,000 feet for a short time with an aircraft gross weight of approximately 85,000 pounds. The aircraft would be accelerated from Mach 3.2 to Mach 3.5 at an altitude of 80,000 feet, then zoomed to

95,000 feet, with speed decaying back to approximately Mach 3.2. The aircraft would subsequently settle back to an altitude of 84,000 feet. Factors which limit sustained flight at altitudes above 85,000 feet are wing area and total thrust. It would be possible to replace the

Each Blackbird uses a 40-foot diameter drag chute that is housed in a compartment on the top of the rear fuselage. A smaller 42-inch diameter pilot chute comes out first and pulls a 10-foot diameter "extraction chute" which in turn deploys the main chute. To prevent the possibility of damage to the vertical stabilizers, the drag chute is normally jettisoned when the aircraft decelerates to 55 knots. (Tony Landis Collection)

The KC-135Q fleet has been disbursed and the few remaining Blackbirds use whatever tanker comes up in the rotation. Here one of the Air Force's reactivated Blackbirds (64-17971) takes on fuel from a KC-135R. (Tony Landis Collection)

outer wing panels with larger ones to provide additional wing surface area, allowing sustained flight above 85,000 feet. However, increasing available thrust would require a new power plant and a total redesign of the inlet, both considered prohibitively expensive.

POSTCRIPT

Even as complex and highly sophisticated as the Blackbird was, at one point it went 17 straight years without a single accident. Six of the 15 OXCARTs built were written off, as were two of the three YF-12As. Over the thirty years that the SR-71 flew for the Air Force, eleven were lost: four of the six test aircraft; the second SR-71B; and six operational SR-71As. None of these were lost to enemy action.

The nineteen Blackbird losses were: one A-12 (60-6929) ran out of fuel in-flight; another A-12 (60-6928) was lost because its flight controls were reversed during maintenance; a single A-12 (60-6939) crashed while landing at Groom Lake due to a hydraulic failure; the second M-21 (60-6941) had a mid-air collision with its D-21 drone; one A-12 (60-6926) and four SR-71As (61-17953, 17966, 17969, and 17970) were lost in pitch-up accidents; the first YF-12A (60-6934) was written-off in a landing accident; the third YF-12A (60-6936) suffered a major in-flight fire; three SR-71As (64-17950, 17954, and

Much has been made in the popular press about the SR-71's "cobra appearance" shown here. The chines proved to be quite successful although Kelly Johnson was originally not terribly impressed with the concept. (Tony Landis Collection)

17977) were lost when a wheel or tire failed on take-off; a single A-12 (60-6932) and SR-71A (64-17953) disintegrated in-flight for unknown reasons at speeds greater than Mach 3; the second SR-71B (64-17957) lost electrical power while landing at Beale AFB; one SR-71A (64-17974) ran off the runway at Kadena in strong winds; and the last SR-71 loss (64-17974) was lost due to a catastrophic in-flight engine failure. Out of all these losses only four crew members lost their lives: Ray Torick in the M-21; Jack Weeks in an A-12 (60-6932); Walt Ray in an A-12 (60-6929); and Jim Zwayer in an SR-71A (64-17952).

The SR-71's record of achievement is untouchable by any known aircraft. 53,490 total flight hours during 17,300 missions flown. Of these, 11,008 hours were accumulated during 3,551 operational reconnaissance missions over North Korea, North Vietnam, the Middle East, South Africa, Cuba, Nicaragua, Iran, Libya, and the Falkland Islands. And demonstrating why it was built in the first place, 11,675 of these hours, including 2,752 during actual operations, were spent above Mach 3. The fleet needed 25,862 in-flight refuelings, mainly by KC-135Qs.

A total of 389 people experienced the thrill of flying over Mach 3 in the Blackbird: 284 were assigned crew members, and 105 were "VIP" guests. The Air Force qualified 93 pilots and 89 RSOs, and LtCol Joseph T. "JT" Vida accumulated 1,492.7 hours, the most by any crew member. Of these crew members, 163 managed to accumulate over 300 hours in the Blackbird, 69 made it to 600 hours, 18 to 900 hours, but only eight accumulated over 1,000 hours.

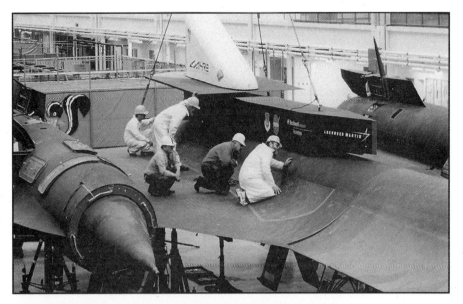

One of the first major experiments identified for the NASA SR-71 was in support of the Lockheed-Martin Reusable Launch Vehicle (RLV) program. A 10% scale model of the Rocketdyne linear aerospike engine will be flight tested prior to the first flight of the X-33 RLV demonstrator vehicle in 1999. Flight testing during the LASRE program is being performed to obtain performance data for an installed aerospike engine at actual flight conditions. (NASA / DFRC)

On 20 December 1989, an SR-71A made a final pass down the Burbank runway to honor all those who worked in designing and producing the fastest air-breathing aircraft in the world. Kelly Johnson, long retired, and gravely ill, was there to watch. He would pass away almost exactly a year later, on 21 December 1990, forever a legend like the aircraft he created.

ACRONYMS

ANGEL
Internal code-name for U-2 project

ARCHANGEL
Internal code-name for early Blackbird designs

AREA 51
Groom Lake, NV

BETA-120
Titanium alloy used to construct the Blackbirds

BLACK SHIELD
Code-name for A-12 operations

BOB
Bureau of the Budget

BOMARC
Air Force air-to-surface missile

CEP
Circular Error Probability (how close to target)

COLD WALL
Name of research project at FRC

DET
Detachment

DEW LINE
Distant Early Warning radar stations in Alaska and Canada

DFRC
NASA Dryden Flight Research Center

DIA
Defense Intelligence Agency

DMZ
Demilitarized Zone (Vietnam)

DoD
Department of Defense

FAN SONG
Code-name for SA-2 SAM guidance radar

FISH
Code-name for Convair parasite aircraft

FRC
NASA Flight Research Center (now DFRC)

FY
Fiscal Year

GUSTO
Code-name for "stealth" aircraft studies

HABU
A snake native to Okinawa; also name applied to SR-71 and its crews

IRIDIUM
The 77th element; name of Motorola satellite project

IRST
Infra-Red Search and Tracking system/sensors

JP
Jet Propellant (JP-4/5/7)

KEDLOCK
Code-name for YF-12A project

KINGFISH
Code-name for Convair competitor to ARCHANGEL

LASRE
Linear Aerospike SR-71 Experiment

NACA
National Advisory Committee on Aeronautics (now NASA)

NASA
National Aeronautics and Space Administration

NIKE HERCULES
U.S. air-to-surface missile

NRO
National Reconnaissance Office

OXCART
CIA code-name for A-12 Blackbirds (aircraft and project)

PINE TREE
Code-name for radar installations in Canada

RAF
Royal Air Force

REX
Code-name for hydrogen engine project

SAC
Strategic Air Command

SAM
Surface-to-Air Missile

SEA
South-East Asia

SENIOR BOWL
Code-name for D-21/B-52 drone program

SENIOR KING
Code-name for SR-71 modernization project

SRS
Strategic Reconnaissance Squadron

SRW
Strategic Reconnaissance Wing

SUNTAN
Code-name for liquid hydrogen-powered aircraft studies

TAGBOARD
Code-name for D-21/M-21 program

TEB
Triethylborane (igniter for JP-7)

THE RANCH
Groom Lake, NV

THE TEST SITE
Groom Lake, NV

SIGNIFICANT DATES

18 OCTOBER 1956
Air Force cancels REX hydrogen-fueled engine project

24 DECEMBER 1957
First J58 engine run

21 APRIL 1958
First mention of ARCHANGEL in Kelly Johnson's dairy

DECEMBER 1958
CIA requests funding for Mach 3+ reconnaissance aircraft program

29 AUGUST 1959
Lockheed and Convair submit proposals for Mach 3+ reconnaissance aircraft

14 SEPTEMBER 1959
CIA awards first ARCHANGEL research contract to Lockheed

26 JANUARY 1960
CIA orders 12 A-12 OXCART aircraft

FEBRUARY 1960
Lockheed begins search for 24 pilots for the A-12

1 MAY 1960
Francis Gary Powers is shot down in a U-2 over the Soviet Union

26 FEBRUARY 1962
First A-12 leaves Burbank for Groom Lake by truck

25 APRIL 1962
First flight of A-12 (60-6924) with Lockheed test pilot Lou Schalk

30 APRIL 1962
First "official" flight of A-12 (60-6924) with Lockheed test pilot Lou Schalk

2 MAY 1962
A-12 goes supersonic (Mach 1.1) for first time during second test flight

13/14 JUNE 1962
SR-71 mock-up reviewed by Air Force

30 JULY 1962
J58 completes pre-flight testing

OCTOBER 1962
Letter of Intent for $1 million for AF-12 (YF-12) delivered to Lockheed

5 OCTOBER 1962
A-12 flies with J75 (left nacelle) and J58 (right nacelle) engines

10 OCTOBER 1962
Skunk Works receives authorization for Q-12 (D-21 drone) study from CIA

28 DECEMBER 1962
Lockheed signs contract to build six SR-71 aircraft

15 JANUARY 1963
A-12 first flight with two J58 engines

24 MAY 1963
First A-12 crashes (60-6926) near Wendover, UT

20 JULY 1963
First A-12 flight over Mach 3

7 AUGUST 1963
First flight of YF-12 (60-6934) with Lockheed test pilot James Eastham

NOVEMBER 1963
A-12 reaches design speed (Mach 3.2) and altitude (78,000 feet)

3 FEBRUARY 1964
A-12 cruises at Mach 3.2 and 83,000 feet for 10 minutes

29 FEBRUARY 1964
President Johnson announces existence of A-11 (actually YF-12)

1 APRIL 1964
M-21 (60-6940) first flight

16 APRIL 1964
First XAIM-47 ejected from YF-12 in flight

JUNE 1964
Final A-12 (60-6939) delivered to Groom Lake

19 JUNE 1964
Fit check of mating of M-21 (60-6940) and D-21(#504)

25 JULY 1964
President Johnson makes public announcement of SR-71

29 OCTOBER 1964
SR-71 (64-17950) prototype delivered to Palmdale

7 DECEMBER 1964
Beale AFB, CA announced as base for SR-71

22 DECEMBER 1964
First flight of SR-71 (64-17950) with Lockheed test pilot Bob Gilliland at Palmdale

22 DECEMBER 1964
First flight M-21/D-21 at Groom Lake with Lockheed test pilot Bill Park

27 JANUARY 1965
A-12 flown for 1 hour and 40 minutes above Mach 3.1 for a distance of 3,000 miles

18 MARCH 1965
First firing of YAIM-47 from YF-12A

1 MAY 1965
Two YF-12A (60-6934 & 6936) set speed and altitude records

28 SEPTEMBER 1965
GAR-9 fired from YF-12A at Mach 3.2 at 75,000 feet

5 MARCH 1966
First launch of a D-21 (#503) from M-21 (60-6941), and flew 150 NM

SIGNIFICANT DATES

30 JULY 1966
Fourth launch of a D-21 (#504) from M-21 (60-6941) results in the D-21 colliding with the M-21, ending M-21/D-21 program

28 DECEMBER 1966
Decision is made to terminate A-12 operations by 1 June 1968

22 MAY 1967
First A-12 (60-6937) flown to Kadena AB by CIA pilot Mel Vojovodich

29 MAY 1967
BLACK SHIELD unit declared operational at Kadena AB

31 MAY 1967
First A-12 (60-6937) operational mission over North Vietnam lasted 3 hours 39 minutes

2 JULY 1967
Jim Watkins and Dave Dempster flew first international sortie in SR-71A (64-17972) when the INS failed on a training mission and they accidentally flew into Mexican airspace

3 NOVEMBER 1967
A-12 and SR-71 conduct a reconnaissance fly-off – Results were inconclusive

5 JANUARY 1968
Skunk Works receives official notice closing down YF-12 operations

23 JANUARY 1968
First A-12 overflight of North Korea during Pueblo incident with CIA pilot Frank Murray

5 FEBRUARY 1968
Lockheed ordered to destroy A-12, YF-12, and SR-71 tooling

8 MARCH 1968
First SR-71A (64-17978) arrives at Kadena AB to replace A-12s

21 MARCH 1968
First SR-71(61-17976) operational mission flown from Kadena AB over Vietnam

8 MAY 1968
Last A-12 Operational mission flown (over North Korea)

29 MAY 1968
CMSGT Bill Gormick starts tie-cutting tradition of Habu crews neck-ties

9 NOVEMBER 1969
First operational D-21 (#517) mission launched from SENIOR BOWL B-52

11 DECEMBER 1969
NASA's first YF-12 (60-6935) flight

20 MARCH 1971
Fourth and last operational D-21 (#527) mission launched from B-52H and flew 2,935 NM

23 JULY 1971
D-21 program cancelled

3 DECEMBER 1974
First flight of SR-71A (64-17959) in "Big Tail" configuration

JANUARY 1975
Clarence "Kelly" Johnson retires as head of the Skunk Works

20 APRIL 1976
TDY operations started at RAF Mildenhall in SR-71A (64-17972)

27 JULY 1976
SR-71A sets 100KM Closed Course World Speed Record at 2,092 MPH

7 NOVEMBER 1979
Last YF-12A (60-6935) flown to Air Force Museum at Wright-Patterson AFB

AUGUST 1980
Honeywell starts conversion of analog flight & inlet control system (AFICS) to digital automatic flight & inlet control system (DAFICS)

15 JANUARY 1982
SR-71B (64-17956) flies it's 1,000th sortie

22 NOVEMBER 1989
Air Force SR-71 program officially terminated

21 JANUARY 1990
Last SR-71 (64-17962) left Kadena AB. Tail art was a tombstone which read: "Det 1 RIP 1968-1990"

26 JANUARY 1990
SR-71 is decommissioned at Beale AFB, CA

6 MARCH 1990
Last flight of the SR-71A (64-17972) sets four world speed records

22 DECEMBER 1990
Clarence "Kelly" Johnson dies at the age of 80

25 JULY 1991
SR-71B #956 (NASA #831) officially delivered to NASA Dryden

OCTOBER 1991
Marta Bohn-Mayer becomes first female SR-71 crew-member

28 SEPTEMBER 1994
Congress votes to allocate $100 million for reactivation of three SR-71s

26 APRIL 1995
First reactivated SR-71A (64-17971) (ex-NASA #832) makes "maiden" flight after being refurbished by Lockheed

28 JUNE 1995
First reactivated SR-71 (64-17971) returns to Air Force inventory

28 AUGUST 1995
Second reactivated SR-71A (64-17967) makes "maiden" flight after being refurbished by Lockheed